Dark Feminine Energy

Nine Powerful Ways to Awaken Your Femme Fatale

Sofia De Paulo

Contents

Introduction

The iconic femme fatale, a French term literally translating to "fatal woman," has captivated the world's imagination for centuries. She is a force to be reckoned with, a woman who is at once powerful, mysterious, alluring, and dangerous. The femme fatale has long symbolized feminine power, independence, and seduction. But more than that, she represents the darker, more complex side of femininity – the side that is often suppressed, ignored, or misunderstood.

In this groundbreaking book, we will explore the essence of the femme fatale and teach you how to unlock your own inner femme fatale. My goal is to help you embrace the full spectrum of your feminine energy and harness it to transform your dating and love life, as well as your relationships with others and, most importantly, with yourself. You will learn how to tap into the magnetic, enchanting, and sometimes-dangerous persona of the femme fatale to create your own captivating and irresistible aura.

As you delve into the pages of this book, you will come to understand what it means to be a femme fatale and how embracing this powerful archetype can unlock new levels of confidence, sensuality, and seduction in your life. This book is designed for women who are ready to explore their darker, more enigmatic side and who are unafraid of embracing their power and seduction to transform their lives.

The purpose of this book is to empower you with the tools and knowledge necessary to embody the characteristics and energy of a femme fatale. You will learn how to balance your dark and light feminine energies, unlocking your full potential and opening the door to a more fulfilling, passionate, and satisfying life. By embracing your dark and light aspects, you can achieve a harmonious balance, accessing the divine feminine within and allowing your true self to shine.

We will delve into the history and mythology of the femme fatale, exploring her role in literature, art, and popular culture. Through this exploration, you will learn how the femme fatale has evolved over time and how she remains a symbol of power and mystique in a world that often seeks to suppress and control feminine energy.

One of the most significant aspects that sets this book apart from others on the market is its commitment to using authentic, evidence-based psychology to guide you in embracing the femme fatale attitude. Rather than relying on empty anecdotes, manipulation, or superficial advice, I have drawn on well-established psychological theories and therapies to provide you with the tools and knowledge necessary for genuine personal transformation. This book is grounded in solid research, with expert-approved insights that empower you to make lasting changes from the inside out.

I have incorporated elements from cognitive behavior therapy (CBT), attachment theory, and various self-improvement therapies to create a comprehensive and effective guide for developing the femme fatale mindset. By utilizing these principles, I aim to help you make lasting changes in your thoughts, behavior, and relationships, ultimately leading you to embody the femme fatale attitude and live a more fulfilling, empowered life.

Many books in this genre focus solely on aesthetics and outward appearances. While these aspects can be crucial in cultivating a femme fatale persona, true transformation must come from within. As the saying goes, a parrot that can mimic a human doesn't mean it's a human. The same principle applies here: simply dressing the part or mimicking the behaviors of a femme fatale will not lead to genuine transformation. In this book, our goal is to help you unleash your inner femme fatale, fostering true and lasting change from within.

But why is it important to embrace both our dark feminine energy? The truth is that, as women, we are multifaceted beings with a rich and complex emotional landscape. By acknowledging and embracing both the dark and light aspects of our feminine energy, we can tap into our full potential and become more authentic, powerful, and magnetic individuals.

Sensuality, intuition, mystery, and power characterize the dark feminine energy. It is the part of us that is daring, seductive, and unapologetic in its desires. The light feminine energy, on the other hand, is nurturing, compassionate, and empathetic. It represents our capacity for love, connection, and emotional intelligence. Both of these energies are vital to our well-being and success in life, and learning to balance them is the key to unlocking our divine feminine power.

In today's world, where women are often encouraged to suppress their dark feminine energy in favor of a more palatable, socially acceptable version of themselves, embracing our entire spectrum of feminine power is more important than ever. By doing so, we can break free from societal expectations and live our lives authentically and unapologetically. Embracing our inner femme fatale allows us to challenge the status quo, redefine what it means to be a woman, and reclaim our rightful place as powerful, magnetic, and seductive beings.

In embracing your inner femme fatale, you will learn to love and accept all parts of yourself, both the dark and light aspects, and in doing so you will be able to create deeper connections with others, attract the love and passion you desire, and live a life that is true to your authentic self. You will discover that you are capable of achieving great things, both personally and professionally, and that your unique combination of dark and light feminine energies can propel you to new heights of success, happiness, and fulfillment.

As you journey through this book, you will be guided and supported every step of the way. We encourage you to be bold, be daring, and embrace the power that lies within you. The world needs more women who are unafraid to tap into their inner femme fatale – women who are confident, sensual, and powerful and who are not afraid to challenge the status quo.

Are you ready to unlock your inner femme fatale and embrace your complete spectrum of feminine power? If so, we invite you to join us on this transformative journey and discover the captivating, alluring, and irresistible woman that lies within you!

Welcome to the world of the femme fatale. Your journey to self-discovery, empowerment, and seduction starts here.

Chapter 1

Understanding Dark Feminine Energy

In this chapter, we will explore the concept of dark feminine energy and its embodiment in the figure of the femme fatale.

As we journey through the realms of history, literature, and pop culture, we will explore examples of femme fatales and uncover the power and allure of the archetype.

What is Feminine Energy?

Feminine energy represents a range of qualities traditionally associated with the female essence. This includes attributes such as nurturing, sensitivity, intuition, creativity, and emotional intelligence.

In today's fast-paced and highly competitive world, understanding and embracing feminine energy can be a powerful tool in personal growth, self-help, and the dating scene. Tapping into your inner femme fatale involves harnessing your inherent feminine energy, allowing you to embody confidence, allure, and magnetism. By understanding the key aspects of feminine energy, you can unlock your true potential in various parts of life, including relationships, personal development, and self-expression.

It's important to note that feminine energy is not exclusive to women; men can also possess and express these qualities. It is a vital counterpart to masculine energy, creating a balance that fosters harmony and growth.

What is Light Feminine Energy?

Light feminine energy encompasses the gentler, more nurturing side of femininity, radiating warmth, understanding, and support. It plays a vital role in creating harmonious relationships and fostering personal growth, both within oneself and in the lives of others. By embracing and cultivating light feminine energy, individuals can foster a sense of connection, compassion, and positive change in various aspects of their lives.

Let's explore some of the attributes associated with light feminine energy:

- **Compassion:** Light feminine energy is characterized by a deep sense of compassion, allowing individuals to empathize with the struggles and challenges faced by others. This heartfelt understanding can lead to stronger, more authentic connections and promote emotional healing and growth.
- **Empathy:** Embracing light feminine energy involves developing a heightened sense of empathy, which enables individuals to attune to the emotions and needs of others. This emotional intelligence allows for better communication, conflict resolution, and emotional support in relationships.
- **Unconditional love:** Light feminine energy is closely tied to the concept of unconditional love, which refers

to loving and accepting others without judgment or expectations. This selfless love creates a supportive and nurturing environment that fosters growth, healing, and emotional well-being.

- **Healing:** The nurturing and compassionate nature of light feminine energy promotes healing on various levels, including emotional, mental, and spiritual. By offering understanding, empathy, and love, individuals can help others overcome challenges and traumas, leading to personal growth and transformation.
- **Support:** Light feminine energy is synonymous with offering support and encouragement, helping others reach their full potential. This can manifest in various ways, from providing emotional support to practical assistance, creating a sense of belonging and unity.
- **Nurturing:** At the heart of feminine energy lies the innate ability to nurture and care for others. This trait is about providing emotional support and creating a safe, loving environment for yourself and those around you. In the context of dating and relationships, nurturing energy can lead to stronger connections and deeper intimacy.
- **Sensitivity:** Feminine energy is often characterized by heightened sensitivity, which allows you to deeply connect with your emotions and the emotions of others. Being in touch with your sensitivity enables you to practice empathy, compassion, and understanding, ultimately leading to more meaningful and fulfilling relationships.

What is Dark Feminine Energy?

Dark feminine energy represents the enigmatic, potent, and captivating aspects of femininity, highlighting the strength and adaptability inherent in the female essence. This energy can be a powerful force for transformation and self-discovery, depending on how it is harnessed and channeled. By understanding and embracing dark feminine energy, individuals can tap into their inner power and cultivate a sense of confidence, magnetism, and resilience.

Let's explore some of the attributes associated with dark feminine energy:

- **Cunning:** Dark feminine energy is characterized by cunning and resourcefulness, allowing individuals to navigate complex situations with ease and intelligence. This skill can be used to overcome challenges, create opportunities, and achieve personal or professional goals.
- **Resilience:** Embracing dark feminine energy involves cultivating a deep sense of resilience, enabling individuals to bounce back from setbacks and adversity. This inner strength and determination can be a powerful driving force for personal growth and transformation.
- **Sensuality:** Dark feminine energy is closely tied to sensuality and the ability to appreciate and express one's physical and emotional desires. By embracing this aspect of femininity, individuals can cultivate a deeper connection with their own bodies and emotions, as well as enhance their romantic relationships.
- **Manipulation:** Dark feminine energy can manifest in the ability to manipulate situations and people to one's advantage. This skill is neither inherently good nor bad; it depends on the intentions and ethics of the individual employing it. When used wisely and

responsibly, it can help individuals navigate social dynamics and achieve their objectives.

- **Intuition:** The mysterious nature of dark feminine energy is often linked to a heightened sense of intuition and the ability to perceive hidden truths. This keen insight can be invaluable in understanding people and situations on a deeper level, allowing individuals to make more informed decisions and respond effectively to challenges.
- **Magnetism:** Dark feminine energy exudes a sense of magnetism and allure that can captivate and influence others. By tapping into this energy, individuals can enhance their self-confidence and personal power, making them more attractive and influential in various aspects of life.
- **Transformation:** Dark feminine energy is a potent force for personal transformation, encouraging individuals to face their shadows, overcome fears, and embrace their true selves. This process of self-discovery can lead to profound personal growth and a deeper understanding of one's own power and potential.

Harnessing dark feminine energy involves exploring the mysterious, powerful, and seductive side of femininity and channeling this energy to achieve personal and professional goals. By embracing and cultivating these aspects of dark feminine energy, individuals can unlock their inner power, resilience, and magnetism, ultimately fostering a greater sense of self-awareness, confidence, and personal growth.

Why Should You Embrace Your Dark Feminine Energy?

Throughout history, patriarchal societies have often sought to maintain power structures that favor men and marginalize women. This imbalance has led to the undervaluation of women and the suppression of their dark feminine energy, which is perceived as a threat to the established order. The power and resilience inherent in dark feminine energy challenge traditional gender roles and expectations, making it a target for suppression.

In patriarchal societies, women are often encouraged to conform to the archetype of the submissive, nurturing, and selfless caregiver. This light feminine energy, while essential and valuable in its own right, is often promoted at the expense of women's darker, more assertive qualities. Women who exhibit dark feminine energy traits such as independence, sensuality, and cunning are often labeled as "difficult," "dangerous," or "unfeminine," leading many to internalize these judgments and suppress their full range of feminine power.

This suppression of dark feminine energy not only limits women's personal growth and self-expression but also perpetuates harmful stereotypes and perpetuates gender inequality. When society forces women into a narrowly defined role, it denies them the opportunity to explore and embrace their full potential, both as individuals and as contributors to the broader community. This confinement to light feminine energy can leave women feeling stuck, unable to access the strength and resourcefulness that can be found within their darker aspects.

Moreover, the suppression of dark feminine energy can have negative consequences for men as well. When women are discouraged from embracing their full range of feminine power, men are left without the opportunity to learn from and appreciate these qualities. This perpetuates a cycle of misunderstanding and fear, which prevents both sexes from achieving true emotional and spiritual balance.

In order to challenge these patriarchal values and create a more equitable society, it is essential for women to reclaim and embrace their dark feminine energy. By recognizing the value and power inherent in these qualities, women can begin to break free from the constraints imposed by traditional gender roles and forge their own paths.

What is the Link Between Femme Fatales and Dark Feminine Energy?

A femme fatale represents the embodiment of dark feminine energy. She is a seductive, powerful, and independent figure who navigates the world with confidence and cunning. Through her allure and intelligence, she is able to influence situations and people to her advantage. The femme fatale embraces her dark energy, harnessing it to achieve her desires and maintain control over her destiny.

One of the most distinctive qualities of femme fatales is their ability to use their allure and seduction to influence others. Dark feminine energy is closely tied to sensuality and magnetism, allowing femme fatales to captivate those around them. This power of attraction enables them to navigate social situations with ease and create opportunities that may not have been available to them otherwise.

Femme fatales often exhibit a strong sense of self-reliance and resilience, which is another manifestation of dark feminine energy. They are not afraid to face challenges head-on and are able to adapt to changing circumstances with grace and determination. This inner strength allows them to maintain control over their lives and make choices that align with their desires and goals.

Dark feminine energy is also closely linked to emotional intelligence and the ability to read and influence the emotions of others. Femme fatales are masters of manipulation, using their emotional acuity to guide situations and people to serve their purposes. They are often able to recognize vulnerabilities in others and exploit them to their advantage, making them formidable opponents and allies.

Femme fatales embody the balance between light and dark feminine energy, which is essential for personal growth and self-discovery. They are able to access their nurturing, compassionate side when necessary, but they are also unafraid to embrace their darker, more assertive qualities. This duality allows them to navigate the complexities of life with a unique blend of grace and power.

Learning From the Best Femme Fatales

Throughout history, literature, pop culture, and real life, the captivating figure of the femme fatale has intrigued and inspired countless generations. These enigmatic women, with their irresistible charm, intelligence, and seductive power, have left an indelible mark on the collective imagination.

You will soon realize these women share the same traits. These women are cunning, resilient, and have the ability to manipulate situations in their favor. By understanding the qualities that define these femme fatales, we can begin to appreciate the allure and power they possess and the ways in which they have shaped the world around them.

After reading this chapter, I encourage you to delve deeper into the lives of these remarkable women, seeking out information about them, watching videos of their performances, and immersing yourself in their stories. As you explore, you will uncover the secrets that lie behind their magnetic personas, learning valuable lessons about the art of seduction, self-confidence, and personal transformation.

Femme Fatales in History

These historical femme fatales showcase the enduring power and allure of dark feminine energy. Their stories illustrate the complex interplay between seduction, ambition, and resilience, offering valuable lessons for those seeking to embrace their own inner femme fatale.

- **Cleopatra:** The last Pharaoh of Ancient Egypt used her intelligence, charm, and beauty to maintain her power and form strategic alliances with powerful men like Julius Caesar and Mark Antony.
- **Lucrezia Borgia:** The daughter of Pope Alexander VI, Lucrezia Borgia was an influential figure during the Italian Renaissance. Known for her beauty, intelligence, and alleged involvement in her family's political intrigues and crimes, she has been portrayed as a cunning femme fatale who used her charm to manipulate powerful men.
- **Josephine Baker:** An American-born French entertainer, Josephine Baker rose to fame during the Jazz Age as a dancer, singer, and actress. Her seductive performances and bold persona made her an icon of the era. During World War II, she also worked as a spy for the French Resistance, using her celebrity status to gather information on the Axis powers.
- **Nell Gwyn:** As a mistress of King Charles II of England, Nell Gwyn was an influential figure in the 17th-century British court. She rose from humble beginnings as an orange seller to become a celebrated actress and the king's favorite consort. Her wit, charm, and beauty helped her maintain her position and influence at court.

Femme Fatales in Literature

These literary femme fatales embody the power and allure of dark feminine energy, often using their seduction and manipulation skills to achieve their goals, whether they be personal, political, or financial.

- **Rebecca de Winters:** The titular character of Daphne du Maurier's novel "Rebecca" is a haunting femme fatale who uses her beauty, charm, and s nature to impact the lives of the characters.
- **Carmen:** The protagonist of the famous opera, "Carmen", is a passionate and free-spirited woman who uses her allure to ensnare men,
- **Scarlett O'Hara:** The protagonist of Margaret Mitchell's "Gone with the Wind," Scarlett is a strong-willed and resourceful Southern belle who uses her charm and cunning to survive and thrive during the Civil War.

Femme Fatales in Pop Culture

These femme fatales in pop culture offer a captivating exploration of the dark feminine energy, showcasing the complexity, power, and seduction that can be wielded by these enigmatic women.

- **Catwoman:** From the Batman comic series, this skilled and seductive woman often uses her charm and cunning to outwit her adversaries.
- **Catherine Tramell:** Sharon Stone's portrayal of Catherine Tramell in the film adaptation of "Basic Instinct" brought the literary femme fatale to life, creating an unforgettable and enigmatic character that captivated audiences.

- **Jessica Rabbit:** This character from the film "Who Framed Roger Rabbit?", is a sultry and mysterious woman who uses her sexuality to seduce and manipulate those around her.
- **O-Ren Ishii:** Lucy Liu's character in the Quentin Tarantino film "Kill Bill" is a skilled assassin and yakuza boss who uses her beauty and ruthlessness to dominate her enemies.

Femme Fatales in Real Life

These real-life femme fatales demonstrate the enduring appeal and power of the archetype. By embracing their dark feminine energy, these women have shaped their own destinies, leaving a lasting impact on popular culture and society.

- **Marilyn Monroe:** The iconic actress and sex symbol of the 1950s and 1960s captivated audiences with her beauty, charisma, and vulnerability. Her relationships with powerful men like Joe DiMaggio, Arthur Miller, and allegedly John F. Kennedy, further contribute to her femme fatale persona.
- **Angelina Jolie:** Known for her striking beauty and bold personality, Jolie has portrayed several femme fatale characters in films such as "Gia," "Mr. & Mrs. Smith," and "Wanted." Her humanitarian work and personal life, including her relationship with Brad Pitt, have also garnered significant attention.
- **Dita Von Teese:** This modern-day burlesque performer and model is famous for her vintage-inspired glamor and seductive stage presence. Dita Von Teese embodies the femme fatale with her sultry performances, elaborate costumes, and confident demeanor.

- **Elizabeth Taylor:** The legendary actress was known for her violet eyes, multiple marriages, and captivating performances in films like "Cleopatra" and "Cat on a Hot Tin Roof." Her tumultuous love life, including her two marriages to Richard Burton, contributed to her femme fatale mystique.
- **Rihanna:** As a singer, actress, and fashion icon, Rihanna exudes confidence, sensuality, and strength. Her bold fashion choices, provocative music, and unapologetic attitude embody the essence of a modern-day femme fatale.
- **Monica Bellucci:** As an Italian actress Monica Bellucci's portrayal of femme fatales is marked by a distinct blend of sensuality, intelligence, and mystery. Her characters often possess a certain enigmatic quality that leaves men spellbound and unable to resist their charms. Bellucci's gaze, husky voice, and graceful movements all contribute to her portrayal of the quintessential femme fatale. In films such as "Irreversible" and "Malèna" Bellucci showcases her ability to command the screen with her sultry presence and seductive power. Her characters often operate on the fringes of society, navigating complex relationships and dangerous situations with ease. Whether she's a villain or a hero, Bellucci's portrayal of the femme fatale is always compelling, captivating, and unforgettable.

What Can We Learn from these Women?

These iconic femme fatales from history, literature, and pop culture share several key traits that reflect the power and magnetism of dark feminine energy.

Let's explore what these key traits are:

- **Intelligence and Cunning:** These women demonstrate exceptional intelligence and cunning, allowing them to navigate complex situations and achieve their goals. Cleopatra is an excellent example of a femme fatale who displayed remarkable intelligence and cunning. As the ruler of a powerful and influential kingdom, she faced numerous challenges and threats to her rule. She used her intellect, charm, and political acumen to form strategic alliances with some of the most powerful men of her time, such as Julius Caesar and Mark Antony.

- **Charm and Seduction:** Each of these femme fatales uses their charm and seductive powers to attract and influence others. Josephine Baker exemplified charm and seduction in her performances and personal life. One of the key elements of her appeal was her ability to combine sensuality with humor, creating an irresistible allure that captivated audiences worldwide. Her playful and provocative performances, often involving extravagant costumes and intricate dance routines, showcased her charisma and ability to charm those around her.

- **Resilience and Determination:** These women display remarkable resilience and determination in the face of adversity, overcoming obstacles and setbacks to maintain their power and influence. Scarlett O'Hara, exemplified resilience and determination throughout the Civil War and its aftermath. Despite facing immense hardships, including the loss of her home and loved ones, Scarlett remained steadfast in her pursuit of survival and success,

- **Ambition and Drive:** These femme fatales are driven by ambition, striving for power, fame, or influence in their respective domains. Elizabeth Taylor, showed immense ambition and drive in her pursuit of a successful acting career. Despite facing numerous personal challenges, including health issues and tumultuous relationships, Taylor's relentless passion for her craft led to securing her place in Hollywood history.

- **Adaptability and Flexibility:** The femme fatales mentioned above demonstrate an incredible ability to adapt to changing circumstances, using their intelligence, charm, and cunning to navigate various situations. Josephine Baker exhibited adaptability and flexibility by transitioning from her American roots to becoming a beloved entertainer in France, embracing a new culture. Moreover, during World War II, she demonstrated her versatility by working as a spy for the French Resistance, using her celebrity status and connections to gather valuable information.

- **Confidence and Self-Assuredness:** Each of these women exudes confidence and self-assuredness, embracing their unique qualities and strengths. Rihanna, the singer, actress, and fashion icon, consistently exudes confidence and self-assuredness in both her personal and professional life. Her unapologetic attitude, bold fashion choices, and provocative music showcase her unwavering belief in herself and her artistic vision.

Summary

In this chapter, we explored the concept of feminine energy and how both lights and dark feminine energy are two sides of the same coin.

We have discussed how dark feminine energy embodies powerful, seductive, and mysterious qualities. I have highlighted the importance of embracing this energy, which is often suppressed in patriarchal societies that value light feminine energy over assertiveness and independence.

This chapter showcased various examples of femme fatales in history, literature, and pop culture who embody the power and allure of dark feminine energy. It also presented real-life femme fatales who have shaped popular culture and society by embracing their dark feminine energy, including Marilyn Monroe, Angelina Jolie, Dita Von Teese, Elizabeth Taylor, and Rihanna.

Chapter 2

Developing a Magnetic and Alluring Presence

The femme fatale is an enigmatic figure, a woman who is confident, mysterious, and irresistible. She commands attention and turns heads wherever she goes. In this chapter, we will explore the art of developing a magnetic and alluring presence by understanding your unique body type, finding your color season, and choosing a signature hairstyle and makeup look. Let's dive into the world of aesthetics and discover how to create a captivating persona that leaves a lasting impression.

Kibbe Body Types

Kibbe body types are a classification system created by the stylist David Kibbe in the 1980s. This system helps you determine your physical appearance by taking into account your bone structure, facial features, and body composition. There are 13 Kibbe body types, each with its unique set of characteristics and recommended styles.

Understanding your Kibbe body type is essential for femme fatales because it allows you to create a personal style that enhances your natural allure. By choosing clothing and accessories that accentuate your features, you can create a powerful and alluring presence. The femme fatale is a master of seduction, and part of that seduction comes from her ability to showcase her unique beauty and style.

The Kibbe body types are:

- **Dramatic:** Tall, angular, and sharp, featuring a strong and prominent bone structure.
- **Soft Dramatic:** A combination of dramatic angles with added curves and softness, creating a bold yet feminine appearance.
- **Romantic**: Delicate, curvy, and feminine, characterized by a small and rounded bone structure.
- **Theatrical Romantic:** A fusion of romantic softness with added drama, showcasing delicate curves and sharp, refined features.
- **Classic:** Balanced, symmetrical, and poised, presenting a harmonious blend of angular and rounded features.
- **Soft Classic:** A slightly softened classic appearance, blending balance and proportion with gentle curves.
- **Dramatic Classic**: A more structured and angular classic appearance featuring stronger bone structure and sharper lines.
- **Natural:** Relaxed, unpretentious, and effortless, characterized by a strong yet slightly rounded bone structure.
- **Soft Natural:** A gentler natural appearance, blending easygoing lines with subtle curves and femininity.
- **Flamboyant Natural:** Bold and dynamic, featuring an unconstructed and free-flowing silhouette with a strong bone structure.

- **Gamine:** Youthful, energetic, and playful, characterized by a petite frame and a mix of angular and rounded features.
- **Soft Gamine:** A more delicate and softened gamine appearance, showcasing a blend of playfulness and gentle curves.
- **Flamboyant Gamine:** A daring and vivacious gamine look, combining youthful energy with dramatic contrasts and sharp lines.

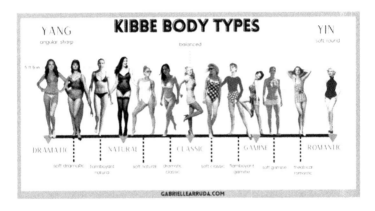

How to Use Kibbe Body Types to Find Your Style

To find your Kibbe body type, you need to take a detailed assessment of your physical attributes. This includes your bone structure, body shape, facial features, and overall balance. Once you've determined your body type, you can then explore the recommended styles and silhouettes that will best complement your unique features.

Here are some general guidelines for each Kibbe body type:

- **Dramatic:** Sharp, geometric lines and bold, structured pieces

- **Soft Dramatic:** A combination of bold shapes with soft, feminine details
- **Romantic:** Soft, rounded shapes and delicate, flowing fabrics
- **Theatrical Romantic:** A mix of romantic elements with added drama and sophistication
- **Classic:** Timeless, balanced styles with clean lines and minimal embellishment
- **Soft Classic:** Classic styles with a touch of softness and subtle femininity
- **Dramatic Classic:** Classic pieces with added structure and sharp detailing
- **Natural:** Relaxed, unconstructed silhouettes with minimal fuss
- **Soft Natural:** Easygoing styles with a hint of softness and femininity
- **Flamboyant Natural:** Bold, unconstructed shapes with an emphasis on movement
- **Gamine:** Youthful, playful styles with clean lines and bold contrasts
- **Soft Gamine:** Gamine styles with added softness and rounded shapes
- **Flamboyant Gamine:** A mix of playful, bold elements with an emphasis on drama

Finding Your Color Season

A true femme fatale knows the power of color and how it can transform her appearance. By choosing colors that complement your natural coloring, you can create a striking and magnetic presence. Wearing the right colors can make your skin glow, your eyes sparkle, and your hair shine. It can also convey confidence, sophistication, and an air of mystery, all of which are essential qualities of a femme fatale.

When choosing the right colors to wear, I suggest researching your "color season". Color season refers to the group of colors that best compliments your skin tone, hair color, and eye color. There are four main color seasons: Winter, Spring, Summer, and Autumn. Determining your color season will help you choose clothing, accessories, and makeup that harmonize with your natural coloring, creating a cohesive and stunning look.

To find your color season, you can consult with a professional color analyst or use online resources and quizzes to guide you through the process. Once you've determined your color season, you'll have a palette of shades that will enhance your natural beauty and contribute to your femme fatale allure.

A basic guide to help you find your color season is as follows:

1. **Determine your undertone:** Examine the veins on the inside of your wrist under natural light. If your veins appear blue or purple, you likely have cool undertones. If your veins appear green or olive, you likely have warm undertones. If it's difficult to determine the color of your veins, you may have neutral undertones.

2. **Assess your hair and eye color:** Consider the natural hue of your hair and the color of your eyes. Individuals with cool undertones typically have ashy, cool-toned hair and blue, green, or gray eyes. Those with warm undertones often have golden, warm-toned hair and brown, hazel, or amber eyes.

3. **Match your undertone and coloring to a season:**

- **Winter:** Cool undertones, high contrast between hair and skin color, and bright or deep eye color. Winters typically look best in bold, cool, and high-contrast colors.

- **Spring:** Warm undertones, light to medium hair and eye color, and a clear or bright overall appearance. Springs usually look best in light, warm, and clear colors.
- **Summer:** Cool undertones, light to medium hair and eye color, and a soft or muted overall appearance. Summers typically look best in soft, cool, and muted colors.
- **Autumn:** Warm undertones, deep or rich hair color, and earthy eye colors. Autumns usually look best in deep, warm, and earthy colors.

Choosing a Signature Hairstyle

Your hairstyle is an essential aspect of your overall look and can significantly impact your allure as a femme fatale. To choose a signature hairstyle, consider the following factors:

- **Your face shape:** Determine your face shape (oval, round, square, heart, or long) and research hairstyles that best suit your features.
- **Your hair type:** Work with your hair's natural texture (straight, wavy, curly, or coily) to find a style that is easy to maintain and enhances your appearance.
- **Your personal style:** Your hairstyle should reflect your personality and complement your wardrobe. Consider your Kibbe body type and color season when choosing a hairstyle.
- **Your lifestyle:** Take into account your daily activities and how much time you have for hair maintenance. Choose a style that fits your schedule and is easy to maintain.

Makeup Choices for a Femme Fatale

Makeup is a powerful tool for creating a captivating and alluring presence. Here are some makeup tips to help you channel your inner femme fatale:

- **Focus on your eyes:** The eyes are the windows to the soul, and a femme fatale knows how to use them to her advantage. Emphasize your eyes with smoky, sultry eyeshadow, winged eyeliner, and dramatic mascara.
- **Flawless complexion:** A smooth, even complexion is essential for creating a polished and sophisticated look. Choose a foundation that matches your skin tone and provides the desired level of coverage. Use concealer to camouflage any imperfections and set your makeup with powder for a long-lasting finish.
- **Sculpted cheeks:** Contouring and highlighting can enhance your bone structure and create a more striking appearance. Use bronzer or contour powder to sculpt your cheekbones, jawline, and temples, and apply a highlighter to the high points of your face.
- **Luscious lips:** Bold, seductive lip colors are a femme fatale's trademark. Opt for deep reds, burgundies, or plums that complement your color season. Alternatively, choose a nude lip color that enhances your natural lip shade for a more understated look.
- Don't **forget your brows:** Well-groomed eyebrows frame your face and add structure to your makeup look. Shape your brows according to your face shape and fill them in with a brow pencil or powder for a polished appearance.

Finding a Signature Fragrance

Finding your signature fragrance as a femme fatale involves a combination of self-discovery, understanding your personal preferences, and selecting a scent that complements your unique persona. The right fragrance should make you feel confident, mysterious, and alluring.

Here are some steps to help you find your signature femme fatale scent:

1. **Reflect on your personality:** Consider the qualities that define you as a femme fatale. Are you bold, seductive, enigmatic, or elegant? Your fragrance should be an extension of your personality and convey your unique essence.
2. **Identify your scent preferences**: Familiarize yourself with the various fragrance families, such as floral, oriental, woody, and fresh. Reflect on the scents you are naturally drawn to and make a list of your favorite notes, such as rose, jasmine, amber, or vanilla.
3. **Research fragrances:** Read fragrance reviews, visit online forums, or consult with knowledgeable sales associates to learn about popular or niche fragrances that align with your preferences and embody the femme fatale persona.
4. **Test fragrances:** Visit a perfume store or order samples online to test different scents on your skin. Allow each fragrance to develop on your skin for a few hours, as the scent may evolve over time. It's essential to experience how a fragrance interacts with your body chemistry before making a decision.
5. **Consider the occasion and season:** As a femme fatale, you may want a versatile fragrance that works well for various occasions or different scents for

specific events. You might also want to consider seasonal variations, opting for a lighter scent in warmer months and a more intense fragrance during cooler months.

6. **Assess the lasting impression:** A femme fatale's signature scent should leave a lasting impression. Pay attention to the longevity and sillage (the trail the fragrance leaves behind) of the scents you test. Choose a fragrance that lasts and subtly captivates the attention of those around you.

7. **Make a confident decision:** Once you've tested various fragrances and found one (or a few) that embody your femme fatale persona, make a confident decision, and start wearing your signature scent. Over time, this fragrance will become synonymous with your presence and enhance your alluring mystique.

Summary

Developing a magnetic and alluring presence as a femme fatale involves understanding your unique physical attributes, finding your color season, and choosing a signature hairstyle and makeup look. By embracing your individuality and using these tools to enhance your natural beauty, you can create a captivating persona that leaves a lasting impression.

Chapter 3

Mastering the Art of Seduction

Unlocking your inner femme fatale involves mastering the art of seduction. This chapter will delve into the different aspects of seduction, with a focus on initial seduction, i.e., attracting the attention of someone you like while in a social gathering. You will be taught how to use your body language, poise, posture, eye contact, and various other tools to effortlessly charm and captivate others. Whether you are shy or outgoing, this guide will help you harness your unique qualities to become an irresistible force.

The Psychology of Body Language

Our body language is a powerful means of communication that can convey subtle yet influential messages. When it comes to seduction, understanding and using body language effectively can create a strong connection between you and your desired partner. By paying attention to your own body language and interpreting that of others, you can create a magnetic presence even from across the room.

Body language plays an essential role in the art of seduction at a party. It allows you to display your confidence, interest, and attraction without saying a word. You do not even have to approach the person so long as you have caught their attention. By being aware of your body language and that of your partner, you can create a powerful connection and establish an unspoken understanding.

Poise and Posture

Embodying the persona of a femme fatale requires a certain level of poise and posture that exudes confidence, allure, and mystery. These qualities are often achieved through a combination of physical presence, body language, and attitude, which together create a magnetic aura that captivates those around you.

Poise refers to the way you carry yourself, your sense of composure, and your ability to handle various social situations with grace and elegance. A femme fatale demonstrates poise by maintaining an air of self-assuredness and remaining unfazed by challenges, which in turn makes her even more intriguing and attractive. Cultivating poise involves practicing mindfulness and self-awareness in social settings, refining your manners, and developing a strong sense of inner confidence.

Posture, on the other hand, is the physical aspect of your presence. An attractive posture can make a significant difference in how you are perceived by others. To achieve the posture of a femme fatale, stand tall with your shoulders back and your head held high. This posture communicates confidence and makes you appear more approachable and attractive. Additionally, maintaining a solid core and engaging your abdominal muscles can help improve your posture, creating a more alluring silhouette.

Facial Expressions

Your facial expressions play a crucial role in capturing someone's attention from across a room or at a party. As a femme fatale, being aware of your facial expressions and using them to your advantage can help you convey emotions and messages that are captivating and alluring.

Here are some tips on how to use facial expressions effectively as a femme fatale trying to catch someone's attention:

- **The power of a smile:** A genuine, warm smile can instantly make you more approachable and attractive. When making eye contact with someone from across the room, a subtle, inviting smile can communicate your interest and encourage them to approach you.
- **The seductive gaze:** Mastering the art of the seductive gaze can be a powerful tool in capturing someone's attention. Hold their gaze with a soft yet intense expression that conveys intrigue and desire. Avoid staring too intensely, as this can be off-putting; instead, opt for a more mysterious and alluring look.
- **Playful expressions:** Incorporate playful facial expressions, such as a raised eyebrow or a coy smirk, to create a sense of intrigue and flirtation. These expressions can convey that you are confident, fun, and engaging, making you even more captivating.
- **The power of mirroring:** Subtly mirroring the facial expressions of the person you are trying to catch the attention of can create a sense of connection and rapport. This can make them feel more drawn to you and enhance your allure.
- **Be mindful of resting expressions:** Ensure that your resting facial expression doesn't convey disinterest or boredom. Maintain an open,

approachable expression that invites others to engage with you, even when you are not actively participating in a conversation.

- **Authenticity is key:** Remember that authenticity is crucial when it comes to facial expressions. Ensure that your expressions align with your genuine emotions and feelings. Forced or exaggerated expressions can come across as insincere and may detract from your allure.

By using your facial expressions effectively, you can create a captivating and alluring presence as a femme fatale, even from across a room or at a party. Remember, the key to capturing someone's attention lies in your ability to communicate your emotions and intrigue through subtle yet powerful non-verbal cues.

Eye Contact

Eye contact plays a crucial role in embodying the persona of a femme fatale. As the saying goes, "The eyes are the window to the soul," and the ability to hold someone's gaze can be an incredibly powerful tool in seduction. Maintaining eye contact communicates interest, trust, and desire and can create a deep, lasting connection between you and your desired partner.

Here are some ways to effectively use eye contact in your journey to becoming a femme fatale:

- **Prolonged gaze:** Holding a steady, prolonged gaze is a classic seduction technique. It shows that you are genuinely interested in the other person and can create a sense of intimacy. When engaging in a conversation, make sure to maintain eye contact for longer intervals, but avoid staring as it may come across as intimidating or uncomfortable.

- **The "triangle technique":** To add a touch of flirtation to your eye contact, use the triangle technique. This involves looking from one of your partner's eyes to the other and then down to their lips. This subtle movement creates a sense of intimacy and can signal romantic interest.

- **Softening your gaze:** A soft, relaxed gaze can be incredibly alluring. Instead of staring intensely, allow your eyes to soften and express warmth and vulnerability. This can make you appear more approachable and open to connection.

- **The power of a lingering glance:** When you catch someone's eye from across the room, hold their gaze for a moment longer than necessary before looking away. This lingering glance can create a sense of intrigue and leave a lasting impression.

- **Smizing:** Smizing, or smiling with your eyes, is a subtle yet powerful way to convey warmth and approachability. To smize, allow the corners of your eyes to crinkle slightly as you smile, creating a genuine and inviting expression.

- **Blinking slowly:** Slow, deliberate blinking can be a subtle yet effective way to communicate your interest and create a sense of connection. By blinking slowly while maintaining eye contact, you can convey a sense of trust and vulnerability.

By incorporating these eye contact techniques into your interactions, you can deepen the connection between you and your desired partner, creating an irresistible sense of attraction. In the world of seduction, the power of eye contact cannot be underestimated. As you continue to develop your femme fatale persona, remember that your eyes can be one of your most potent tools in captivating and enchanting those around you.

Move with Grace

Graceful movements and slinking are distinctive ways of moving that convey elegance, fluidity, and sensuality. These types of movements can significantly enhance one's presence, making them appear more captivating and alluring. Let's dive deeper into what these terms actually mean and how they differ from each other.

- **Graceful movements** are characterized by their smoothness, elegance, and effortlessness. These movements typically flow seamlessly from one to the next, creating a sense of harmony and beauty. Graceful movements often involve the following qualities:
- **Fluidity:** Graceful movements are marked by their continuous and flowing nature, with minimal abruptness or jerkiness.
- **Precision:** There is a sense of intention and control in graceful movements, with each action being executed with accuracy and purpose.
- **Balance:** Graceful movements maintain a sense of equilibrium, even when shifting weight or transitioning between different positions.
- **Elegance:** There is an inherent beauty and refinement in graceful movements, which can be captivating and mesmerizing to watch.

Slinking, on the other hand, is a specific type of graceful movement that is characterized by its sensuality and stealth-like quality. Slinking movements are smooth, fluid and often appear almost serpentine or feline in nature. Some key aspects of slinking include:

- **Subtlety:** Slinking movements are often understated and subtle, allowing the individual to glide through spaces with ease and stealth.
- **Sensuality:** There is an inherent seductiveness in slinking movements, which can be both alluring and captivating.
- **Flexibility:** Slinking often involves a degree of flexibility and suppleness in the body, allowing for smooth and fluid transitions between movements.
- **Control:** Despite their apparent effortlessness, slinking movements require a high level of control and body awareness to execute effectively.

Both graceful movements and slinking involve fluidity, elegance, and control, but slinking is distinguished by its sensual and stealth-like qualities. By incorporating these types of movements into one's physical presence, an individual can create a captivating and alluring persona that is reminiscent of the femme fatale archetype.

Controlled Gestures

Controlled gestures can be an essential aspect of embodying the femme fatale persona, as they help you convey confidence, allure, and intrigue through non-verbal communication. You might assume that in order to catch the attention of someone across the room, you need to make your gestures large. In reality, this can make you look overly performative and obviously trying to attract attention. By using your hands and arms to accentuate your words and expressions in a controlled way, you can enhance your captivating presence.

Here are some tips on how to incorporate controlled gestures as a femme fatale:

- **Keep it natural:** Focus on using gestures that feel natural and authentic to you. Avoid mimicking or exaggerating movements that don't align with your personality, as this can make you appear inauthentic or disingenuous.
- **Be mindful of the context:** Adapt your gestures based on the social setting and the people you are interacting with. In more formal situations, it may be appropriate to use more subtle, refined gestures, while in casual settings, you might opt for more relaxed and expressive movements.
- **Use gestures to emphasize points:** When making a point or telling a story, use controlled gestures to accentuate your words and add emphasis. This can help draw attention to your message and create a more engaging and memorable interaction.
- **Maintain eye contact:** While using gestures, be sure to maintain eye contact with your conversation partner. This can help you establish a connection and convey your confidence and allure as a femme fatale.
- **Balance gestures with stillness:** As a femme fatale, it's essential to strike a balance between using controlled gestures and maintaining moments of stillness and poise. By doing so, you can create an air of mystery and intrigue that captivates those around you.
- **Practice and refine:** To develop effective controlled gestures, take time to practice and refine your movements. Observe others, watch films or videos featuring femme fatale characters, and experiment with different gestures to find the ones that feel most natural and effective for you.

Remember, the key to captivating those around you lies in your ability to communicate effectively, both verbally and non-verbally, and controlled gestures can play a significant role in achieving this.

Summary

In this chapter we delved into the art of seduction, focusing on using body language and other tools to charm and captivate others at a distance.

Key takeaways include:

- Understanding the power of body language,
- Maintaining proper posture and poise,
- Using facial expressions and eye contact effectively,
- Incorporating graceful movements and controlled gestures.

By mastering these aspects, one can embody the femme fatale persona and become an irresistible force in social settings.

Chapter 4

The Art of Conversation

When it comes to dating, one of the most important skills you can develop is the ability to engage in fascinating conversation. Mastering the art of conversation will not only make you more appealing to potential romantic partners but will also boost your confidence and help you unlock your inner femme fatale. In this chapter, we will explore techniques and strategies that will help you excel in conversation and leave a lasting impression on your target.

Tone of Voice

As a femme fatale, your tone of voice is a powerful tool that can be used to draw people in and leave a lasting impression. To truly captivate someone, you need to project confidence, warmth, and charm through your voice. Speak clearly and at a steady pace, ensuring that your words can be easily understood. Remember to vary your pitch and volume to keep the conversation engaging while also paying attention to the tone of the other person to gauge their interest and comfort levels.

A low, sultry voice is often associated with the femme fatale persona. This type of voice conveys a sense of mystery, allure, and sensuality that can be incredibly captivating. To adopt a low, sultry tone, focus on relaxing your vocal cords and speaking from your diaphragm. This will give your voice a more profound, more resonant quality that can create a mesmerizing effect.

Incorporate this sultry voice into your conversations by using it strategically – for example, when sharing a personal story or expressing a thought that you want to emphasize. Be mindful not to overuse this tone, as it can lose its impact if it becomes your default way of speaking. Instead, use it as an accent to punctuate key moments in the conversation, creating a sense of depth and intrigue.

Why Being Shy Can Be a Plus

Contrary to popular belief, shyness can be an attractive quality. In fact, 50% of people rate themselves as shy, and research shows that shyness is often considered an appealing personality trait. Embrace your shyness and use it to create a sense of intrigue and mystique.

Being shy can also allow you to be a better listener, as you're more inclined to focus on the other person's words and thoughts. This can make your conversation partner feel valued and heard, which is a powerful way to build attraction.

However, it's essential not to let your shyness prevent you from engaging in meaningful conversation. Practice striking a balance between being open and vulnerable while also maintaining an air of mystery that keeps your target intrigued.

Mirroring

Mirroring is a subtle technique that can help you build rapport and create a sense of connection with your conversation partner. It involves subtly mimicking their body language, gestures, and speech patterns. By doing this, you can create a sense of familiarity and comfort that will make your target feel more at ease.

To practice mirroring, pay close attention to your target's body language and movements. If they cross their legs, do the same. If they lean in while speaking, mirror this action. Be subtle in your mirroring, as overt mimicry can come across as insincere or even creepy.

Breaking the Touch Barrier

Physical touch can be a powerful way to enhance the connection you're building through conversation. However, it's essential to approach touch with care, as it can also make some people uncomfortable. Start with light, casual touches on the arm or shoulder, and gauge their reaction. If they seem receptive, you can gradually escalate the level of physical contact.

Remember to always be respectful of your target's boundaries and never force physical contact if they seem uncomfortable. By breaking the touch barrier in a gentle and thoughtful way, you can create a sense of intimacy and closeness that will enhance your overall rapport.

Identify Your Target's Favorite Emotion

To truly captivate someone, identify their favorite emotion, and provide them with an experience they have never had before. This can create a deep and lasting impression, making you unforgettable. To do this, pay close attention to their body language, facial expressions, and the stories they share. Look for patterns that indicate which emotions they gravitate toward and try to evoke those emotions in your conversation.

For example, if your target seems to enjoy feeling inspired, share stories of personal triumph or people who have overcome great odds. If they prefer humor, inject wit and playfulness into your conversation. By tailoring your conversation to their emotional preferences, you'll be able to forge a deeper connection.

Giving and Taking

A successful and engaging conversation is a delicate dance between two roles: givers and takers. The best conversations strike a balance between these roles, creating an ebb and flow of ideas, emotions, and connections. Understanding the importance of both roles and learning to navigate between them will help you master the art of conversation.

Givers are individuals who contribute to the conversation by sharing their thoughts, experiences, and opinions. They provide the fuel that keeps the discussion going and often set the tone and direction of the conversation. As a giver, it's important to be aware of the impact your words have on the other person and to strive for a balance between self-expression and sensitivity to your conversation partner's feelings and interests.

A good giver knows when to inject their own experiences and opinions into the conversation while also allowing space for the other person to share their thoughts. They listen actively, ask thought-provoking questions, and demonstrate genuine curiosity about the other person's perspective.

Takers, on the other hand, are the listeners and absorbers in a conversation. They receive the information and stories shared by the giver, processing them and providing feedback, empathy, and understanding. The role of a taker is essential, as they create a safe and comfortable environment for the giver to open up and share their thoughts.

A skilled taker knows how to listen attentively and provide thoughtful responses that encourage the giver to continue sharing. They can also recognize when it's time to switch roles and become the giver, sharing their own experie

In a healthy conversation, both participants fluidly switch between the roles of giver and taker. This creates a dynamic and engaging interaction where each person feels heard, valued, and understood. It's essential to be aware of your natural conversational tendencies – are you more of a giver or a taker? – and to actively work on balancing these roles in your interactions.

Pay attention to the flow of conversation and be mindful of when it's time to switch roles. If you've been sharing your experiences and opinions for an extended period, consider giving your conversation partner an opportunity to speak. Conversely, if you've been mostly listening, take the initiative to share your thoughts and contribute to the discussion.

A successful conversation relies on a delicate balance between givers and takers. By recognizing the importance of both roles and learning to navigate between them, you'll be better equipped to engage in meaningful and enjoyable conversations. This skill will not only help you in your romantic pursuits but also improve your relationships and connections in all aspects of life.

Signs of Disinterest

While mastering the art of conversation can increase your chances of captivating your target, it's important to recognize when someone is not interested in pursuing a deeper connection. Pay attention to their body language, tone of voice, and the content of their responses.

Signs of disinterest may include:

- **Closed body language:** If your target is crossing their arms, avoiding eye contact, or turning their body away from you, these may be signs that they are not engaged in the conversation.
- **Monosyllabic responses:** If they are only providing short, terse answers and not contributing much to the conversation, this may indicate a lack of interest.
- **Frequent glances at their phone or watch:** This can signal that they are eager to wrap up the conversation and move on.
- **Lack of follow-up questions:** If your target doesn't ask questions about your experiences or opinions, it may be a sign that they are not truly invested in getting to know you better.

If you notice these signs of disinterest, it's essential to respect the other person's feelings and gracefully exit the conversation. Remember, not every conversation will lead to a romantic connection, and it's crucial to recognize when it's time to move on. Your time is too precious to spend on a deadened romance; there are plenty of others out there who will find you captivating.

Summary

In this chapter, we discussed how to use conversation to captivate your target. Key takeaways from this chapter include:

1. Use a confident, warm, and charming tone of voice, and occasionally employ a low, sultry voice to captivate your target.
2. Embrace your shyness as an attractive quality and use it to create intrigue and mystique.
3. Practice mirroring to build rapport and connection with your conversation partner.
4. Break the touch barrier gently and thoughtfully to enhance intimacy and closeness.
5. Identify your target's favorite emotion and cater your conversation to evoke that emotion for a deeper connection.
6. Understand the importance of both givers and takers in conversation and learn to navigate between these roles.
7. Recognize signs of disinterest and respect your target's feelings by gracefully exiting the conversation when necessary.

Chapter 5

The Nine Qualities of a Femme Fatale

This chapter is split into nine sections, a section for each quality a femme fatale needs to succeed.

Each section includes a story from my life to help you understand the importance of my message and to let you know that you are not alone. Next is a discussion about why this quality is essential to a femme fatale and some of the issues you may be facing.

Finally, and most importantly, each section ends with practical exercises you can do to enhance these qualities in yourself. These exercises are taken from real psychology and therapy techniques and are designed to rewire your brain.

You may find some of these techniques more challenging than others, as many of them require you to look inside yourself and identify problems and unhelpful thinking patterns. I urge you to complete all of the exercises in this chapter, and I can guarantee that after six to eight weeks, you will feel and see the difference within yourself.

Quality One

She is Mysterious

In this section, we'll explore how femme fatales can cultivate an air of mystery that leaves people wanting more. We'll delve into what it means to be mysterious yet authentic, learning when to share and when to hold back.

Authenticity and mystery might seem like contrasting concepts, but they can coexist harmoniously in the persona of a femme fatale. The key is to strike a balance between openness and discretion, which allows us to present our true selves while maintaining an air of intrigue.

My Story

Once upon a time, long before I became the femme fatale I am today, I was an enthusiastic and chatty young woman named Sofia. I had always been a gregarious person, excited to share every detail of my life with anyone who would listen. I believed that being raw and unfiltered was the truest form of authenticity and that it would help me build genuine connections with others. My belief in the power of openness led me to overshare not only in face-to-face conversations but also on social media.

I used to post everything on Facebook, Instagram, and Twitter. My daily routines, personal opinions, relationship updates, and even the most intimate aspects of my life were available for the world to see. I often shared my vulnerabilities and insecurities in the hope of fostering empathy and solidarity with others. I thought that by being so open, I was making myself relatable and forging bonds with those around me.

One day, I attended a party with a group of friends. It was a vibrant event filled with laughter and conversation. I was in my element, enjoying the opportunity to connect with others and exchange stories. As the night wore on, I found myself in a circle of people, regaling them with tales of my recent dating adventures. I thought my honesty and vulnerability would make me the life of the party, but I couldn't have been more wrong.

As I animatedly recounted my escapades, I noticed that the faces around me started to shift. Smiles turned into polite nods, and laughter faded into an uncomfortable silence. I couldn't understand what was happening. Weren't my stories supposed to bring us closer together? It was at that moment that I caught a glimpse of my reflection in a nearby mirror. I saw myself as I was – a young woman, desperate for validation and attention, oversharing her life without a second thought.

The realization hit me like a ton of bricks. I was coming across as needy, making myself look like a show-off, and ultimately pushing people away. The authenticity I had so prized was not only failing to bring me closer to others but also causing them to dislike me.

It was a sobering moment, and I knew I had to change. I didn't want to be seen as someone who was trying too hard to impress others. I wanted to be someone who could command respect and admiration effortlessly – a femme fatale.

I began my transformation by becoming more mindful of what I shared and with whom. I learned to balance my openness with discretion, choosing to reveal only those parts of myself that would foster genuine connections without overexposing my vulnerabilities. I practiced the art of listening more than speaking, engaging with others' stories and experiences instead of dominating the conversation with my own. I cultivated an air of mystery, only revealing the most intriguing aspects of my life and leaving others eager to learn more.

On social media, I started curating my content, posting less frequently and more thoughtfully. I showcased my growth and accomplishments while sharing moments of vulnerability, but only when they served a purpose or carried a powerful message. In short, I became a more deliberate and conscious version of myself.

This new approach transformed not only my relationships with others but also my relationship with myself. I became more confident, more self-assured, and more capable of attracting the type of people and experiences I truly desired. And so, the journey to becoming a femme fatale had begun.

The Psychology of Mystery

The psychology of mystery, rooted in our innate desire to explore the unknown, plays a significant role in the allure of femme fatales. Their mysterious nature captivates and fascinates, leaving others eager to uncover the secrets they seem to possess. This intrigue is deeply ingrained in human nature, as our ancestors relied on their instincts to identify and navigate unknown environments that could prove to be beneficial or threatening.

Femme fatales embody this sense of mystery, drawing people in with their enigmatic charm and indistinct aura. Their ability to selectively reveal information about themselves creates an air of fascination, which involuntarily captures the attention of those around them. This allure is similar to that of a painting spotted from across a gallery, inviting viewers to step closer and immerse themselves in the intricate details and hidden meanings within the canvas. Much like the painting, the femme fatale beckons others to delve deeper, to become absorbed in the layers of her personality, and to uncover the stories she chooses to share. As people engage with the femme fatale, they find themselves captivated by the enigma she presents, their curiosity piqued by the glimpses of vulnerability and strength that lie beneath her mysterious exterior.

In social contexts, the mysterious nature of femme fatales has several advantages. First, it encourages others to invest time and effort in getting to know them, fostering deeper connections and allowing the femme fatale to maintain control over the relationship dynamic.

Second, their air of mystery often signals an intriguing depth of character, suggesting that they possess valuable knowledge or experiences that others might want to access. This creates a sense of exclusivity and desirability, making the femme fatale an even more attractive figure.

In short, the psychology of mystery plays a crucial role in the appeal of femme fatales. By cultivating an air of intrigue and fascination, they tap into deep-seated human desires to explore the unknown and captivate the attention of those around them. This mysterious quality not only makes femme fatales more attractive but also allows them to foster deeper connections and maintain control over their relationships, embodying the essence of empowerment and self-assuredness.

Mystery and Authenticity

For a femme fatale, authenticity is about embracing her true self and living in harmony with her values. Her words and actions must align with her beliefs in order to maintain her enigmatic charm. However, the notion of authenticity has been somewhat distorted over time. Many people have come to associate "being honest" and "owning your story" with revealing their deepest secrets to the world.

A femme fatale must recognize that using social media as a personal diary or treating casual acquaintances like therapists can have serious consequences.

Sharing too much information with the wrong person might jeopardize her safety. Overexposing her personal life may make others feel uncomfortable, potentially pushing them away. Additionally, discussing her problems with those who lack genuine concern for her well-being could leave her open to exploitation.

By striking a balance between openness and discretion, a femme fatale can maintain her authenticity while preserving her allure, protecting her privacy, and fostering healthy relationships.

Here are some reasons why femme fatales may unintentionally cross the line from authenticity to oversharing:

- Seeking sympathy through misguided means. Sharing your mistakes to help others learn demonstrates authenticity. However, if you disclose your struggles solely to gain pity, you are oversharing.
- Attempting to accelerate relationship development. Authentic individuals prioritize building relationships. Oversharers divulge personal information to create a sense of intimacy without first establishing trust.
- Allowing your story to control you. When pain is fresh, it may feel as though everyone can see your inner turmoil. This sensation can provoke anxiety, prompting some to overshare to alleviate their discomfort. Authentic femme fatales, on the other hand, manage this anxiety and carefully weigh the decision to share their experiences.

By understanding these distinctions, femme fatales can maintain their mysterious allure while remaining authentic in their connections with others.

Becoming a Mysterious Femme Fatale

Now that you understand the psychology behind a mysterious persona and understand that mystery and authenticity are intrinsically linked, it's time to put it into practice. I have provided you with some practical tips on embodying the mysterious energy of the femme fatale for yourself.

To Share Or Not To Share

Before sharing information with others, femme fatales should consider their motivations. Are you confiding in someone about your personal struggles to gain sympathy, or are you sharing with a trusted confidant? Are you disclosing sensitive information to a colleague to help them understand the impact on your performance, or are you revealing private details in hopes of them seeing you as a close ally?

Naturally, there are instances when sharing becomes necessary. Perhaps you need to inform your employer about a personal matter that affects your work schedule or availability. In such cases, it's crucial to communicate your situation.

However, before divulging your personal challenges in a social setting, femme fatales should weigh their reasons and assess the potential consequences. By doing so, they can maintain their enigmatic allure while upholding their authenticity and preserving their privacy.

Strategic Absence

When a femme fatale is always present, people may become overly familiar with her, eventually taking her presence for granted. While building meaningful relationships is essential, cultivating a mysterious energy requires making others yearn for your company.

How can a femme fatale achieve this? First, be present and demonstrate your captivating qualities. Once people begin to appreciate and enjoy your company, you'll undoubtedly be invited out again, but instead of showing up to every social event, practice strategic absence.

Strategic absence is the art of not accepting all your invites. Your excuses can range from being occupied with another task, feeling tired, or you're going away on a trip the next day. Whatever you choose, keep it purposefully vague so as not to give too much away. Occasionally you can say you're going to attend and then not turn up. However, I would avoid this too often as you risk offending people!

If you are genuinely enchanting to be around, others will miss you at these events and inquire about your whereabouts. This strategy allows femme fatales to maintain their enigmatic allure while fostering deeper connections.

Leave the Party Early

A well-timed departure can be a powerful tool in cultivating a femme fatale's mysterious energy. Engaging in captivating conversations and exuding charm, only to make a graceful exit, can leave a lasting impression on those around you.

To execute this strategy effectively, follow these steps:

- **Be attentive and charming:** When you're attending a social gathering or engaging in a conversation, be fully present, and demonstrate your wit, intelligence, and charm. This ensures that your company is genuinely enjoyable and leaves others wanting more.
- **Know when to exit:** Develop an instinct for recognizing when the energy begins to wane or when conversations start to feel repetitive. Leaving at the

right moment allows you to maintain your allure and keep your mysterious energy intact.

- **Excuse yourself with poise:** When it's time to depart, gracefully excuse yourself without drawing too much attention. Offer a genuine reason, if necessary, or simply express your gratitude for the conversation and company.
- **Leave a hint of intrigue:** As you exit, leave a subtle hint of your plans or interests, giving others something to ponder in your absence. This will further enhance your mysterious aura and keep you in their thoughts.

Master the "French Exit"

A French exit, also known as an "Irish goodbye," is the act of leaving a social gathering without announcing your departure or saying goodbye to the host or other guests. It's a discreet way to exit a party or event, often leaving others wondering where you've gone.

In the context of being a mysterious femme fatale, a French exit can contribute to your enigmatic aura in the following ways:

Intrigue: When you leave without notice, people will naturally be curious about your sudden disappearance. This curiosity can create a sense of intrigue and speculation about your actions, adding to your mysterious reputation.

Unpredictability: A French exit demonstrates an unpredictable side to your personality. By keeping others guessing about your next move, you maintain a sense of mystery that makes you more captivating and alluring.

Maintaining control: A French exit allows you to control your exit without getting caught up in lengthy goodbyes or explanations. This level of self-assuredness and autonomy is characteristic of a femme fatale who knows how to navigate social situations with grace and finesse.

Leaving a lasting impression: A well-executed French exit will leave a lasting impression on those present. Your absence will be felt, and your memory will linger in the minds of those you've left behind, making them eager to reconnect with you in the future.

However, it's essential to use the French exit sparingly and with caution. Overuse or inappropriate use can be perceived as rude or disrespectful, which could harm your relationships rather than enhance your mysterious persona.

Note: Remember to thank the host for inviting you over a text message or a phone call. You can say something along the lines of "I'm sorry we didn't get a chance to say goodbye, but I wanted to thank you for inviting me. It was great seeing you; we should definitely do this again!"

Summary

In conclusion, femme fatales embody a sense of mystery, captivating others with their enigmatic charm and selective revelations about themselves. It is a vital aspect of the femme fatale persona. Key takeaways to remember include:

1. Authenticity is not synonymous with oversharing; true authenticity means knowing when to share and when to maintain discretion.
2. Cultivating an air of mystery involves balancing openness with privacy, and nurturing genuine connections without overexposing vulnerabilities.
3. Oversharing can push people away, while a mysterious femme fatale draws them in by being authentic yet intriguing.

4. Utilize strategies such as the French exit and strategic absences to maintain a sense of mystery and leave a lasting impression.
5. Be mindful of the line between being mysterious and being disrespectful or rude, as maintaining healthy relationships is crucial to the femme fatale persona.

Quality Two

She is Humble and Quiet

In this section, we'll explore how femme fatales cultivate a humble and quiet persona by embracing the art of humility. Practicing humility involves understanding our place in the grand scheme of things and recognizing our limitations while appreciating that it is not synonymous with meekness or weakness.

As we embark on the journey toward mastering humility, we'll delve into practical exercises that foster self-awareness and emotional intelligence. These exercises will enable us to form connections built on trust, intimacy, and mutual respect, without losing our unique charm and grace.

My Story

During my early days as a dance studio entrepreneur, I was still navigating the murky waters of self-confidence and the art of presenting oneself. One particular instance still stands out in my memory; a time when my over-enthusiasm about my thriving dance studio made me come across as a braggart.

A couple of years ago, I had started a dance studio that was my pride and joy. I poured my heart and soul into making it a success, and it paid off. Within a short span of time, it had become one of the most popular studios in town, boasting an impressive roster of students and a stellar reputation.

One evening, I attended a networking event for local entrepreneurs. I was eager to share the success of my dance studio with everyone, hoping it would make a lasting impression. As the event progressed, I found myself engaged in conversation with a group of fellow entrepreneurs. I wasted no time in regaling them with tales of how well my dance studio was doing.

I told them about the rapid growth of my student base, the number of dance classes we offered, and how we had already expanded to a larger space to accommodate the demand. I even went into detail about our impressive social media following and the media coverage we had received. While everything I said was true, I didn't realize that my incessant bragging was starting to make me sound unbecoming. Instead of letting the conversation flow naturally and allowing others to share their experiences, I dominated the discussion. I reveled in recounting each accomplishment, growing more animated with every detail. I didn't notice the growing discomfort on my fellow entrepreneurs' faces or the subtle hints that they wanted to change the topic.

As the evening wore on, I continued to monopolize the conversation. Instead of asking questions about others' businesses or showing genuine interest in their stories, I steamrolled ahead, boasting about the accolades my dance studio had received and the celebrities who had attended our classes.

At one point, a woman in the group tried to interject, attempting to share her own experiences with her recently launched fashion boutique. But I quickly interrupted, launching into a new story about the incredible testimonials we had received from our students. The woman's face fell, and the others in the group exchanged uncomfortable glances.

Finally, the event came to a close, and as I said my goodbyes, I couldn't shake the feeling that something was off. It wasn't until later that night when I lay in bed replaying the evening's events, that I realized how obnoxious I must have seemed. Though I was genuinely proud of my accomplishments, I had let my enthusiasm morph into an unattractive display of boasting.

That night was a turning point for me. I understood the importance of humility and how it could make or break one's image. From then on, I made a conscious effort to balance my pride in my achievements with a genuine interest in the stories and successes of others.

In time, I learned to present myself with confidence, grace, and humility, unlocking the inner femme fatale that had been hiding within me all along.

The Art of Humility

At first glance, embracing humility may not seem like the key to unlocking your inner femme fatale. After all, this book focuses on self-esteem and self-worth, urging us to celebrate our achievements and take pride in ourselves. However, humility is not synonymous with meekness or weakness. It's about understanding our place in the grand scheme of things and recognizing our limitations.

Practicing humility involves looking beyond our own desires and fears to understand our role within a broader community and a specific historical moment. In the realm of dating and self-help, embracing humility can lead to more meaningful connections and help us recognize areas where we can grow.

Here is why embracing humility can improve your dating life and help you unlock your inner femme fatale:

- **Enhancing social cohesion and belonging:** Just as Confucius believed in knowing our place in a larger social world, humility can foster a sense of belonging in social situations, making us more approachable and relatable in the dating scene.
- **Avoiding arrogance and pretentiousness:** By adopting a humble mindset, we can avoid coming across as arrogant or pretentious, qualities that can be off-putting to potential partners.
- **Learning from others:** Humility allows us to recognize that we have much to learn from those around us, including our romantic interests. By being open to learning from others, we can become more well-rounded and appealing individuals.
- **Embracing self-improvement:** A humble mindset involves constantly seeking self-correction and self-improvement. By admitting our shortcomings and actively working to overcome them, we become more attractive and authentic partners, capable of growth and self-development.
- **Overcoming narcissism:** In a world where narcissism is increasingly prevalent, embracing humility can serve as an antidote. By focusing less on self-importance and more on genuine connections, we can cultivate deeper, more meaningful relationships.
- **Improving cognitive and interpersonal skills:** Studies have shown that humble individuals have better problem-solving abilities, are more open to feedback, and possess superior interpersonal skills. These traits can significantly enhance our dating experiences and relationships.

- **Fostering trust and engagement:** Humility in our interactions with others, including romantic partners, can foster trust, engagement, and open communication, leading to more satisfying and successful relationships.

By embracing humility, we can unlock our inner femme fatale and improve our dating experiences. It's not about diminishing our self-worth but rather understanding our limitations and embracing a mindset of growth, learning, and genuine connection.

Becoming a Humble Femme Fatale

If you practice humility, you will unlock a quiet confidence and charm, something well sought after in the world of a femme fatale. Here are eleven ways to practice humility:

Allow Others to Speak

As a femme fatale, it's important to exude confidence and self-assuredness. However, in conversations with others, it's equally crucial to allow space for them to express their thoughts and opinions. While it may be tempting to talk about yourself and your accomplishments, resist the urge to make the conversation all about you.

Instead, take an interest in your conversation partner and ask them questions about their life and experiences. Allow them to share their insights and opinions on various topics and be open to learning from their perspective. By giving them a chance to speak, you may discover new ideas and experiences that can broaden your own horizons.

Tip: Consider asking your date which book has had the most significant impact on their life or worldview. This not only provides an opportunity to learn about their interests but also allows them to share a life-changing experience.

Avoid Gossip

As a femme fatale navigating the dating world, it's essential to maintain a sense of dignity and grace in your interactions with others. While hearing gossip and rumors may be inevitable, it's important not to engage in this kind of conversation. Gossip can be incredibly damaging to those involved, and as a strong, confident woman, you have no need for such negative energy.

Instead of giving in to the temptation to indulge in gossip, try to steer the conversation in a more positive direction. Reframe the discussion to focus on more uplifting topics, such as shared interests or experiences. This not only demonstrates your maturity and class but also shows that you value meaningful conversation over superficial drama.

If you find that the other person is insistent on gossiping, don't be afraid to walk away from the conversation. You can always come back to it at a later time or shift your attention to a more enjoyable activity. Remember, as a femme fatale, you have no need for toxic conversations or negative energy in your life.

Tip: Consider cultivating a reputation for being a positive, uplifting presence in your social circles. By demonstrating your disinterest in gossip and drama, you'll attract like-minded individuals who share your values and mindset.

Overlook the Negative Actions of Others

As a femme fatale, it's important to cultivate a sense of empathy and understanding in your relationships with others. While it can be tempting to judge someone for their mistakes or negative actions, this kind of attitude only serves to perpetuate negativity and harm.

Instead of focusing on the faults of others, try to approach them with compassion and understanding. Remember, we've all made mistakes in our lives, and nobody is perfect. By offering your support and care, you can demonstrate your maturity and class and position yourself as a supportive, uplifting presence in their life.

Tip: Try to focus on the positive qualities and actions of others rather than dwelling on their negative traits.

It's Okay If People Don't Like You

As a powerful, confident femme fatale, it's important to remember that not everyone will appreciate or approve of you. In a world where social media dominates our lives and self-worth is often measured by likes and followers, it can be tempting to seek validation from others. However, true strength and confidence come from within, and it's important not to let the opinions of others define you.

If someone doesn't enjoy your company or approve of you, don't take it too seriously. There may be many reasons why someone doesn't connect with you, and most of the time, it has nothing to do with you. Instead, focus on the people in your life who value and appreciate you and who help you grow as a person.

Remember that friendships may come and go, but that doesn't diminish their value. People enter and exit our lives for a variety of reasons, and it's important to appreciate the time we have with those who do choose to be in our lives.

Tip: When posting on social media, focus on documenting your life and experiences rather than seeking validation from others. Seeking the approval of others can be damaging to your self-esteem and can lead to an unhealthy focus on external validation. Instead, focus on being true to yourself and living your life authentically, and the right people will naturally be drawn to you.

Back Down from a Useless Fight

Conflicts are bound to arise among friends and loved ones, a natural part of human interaction. As a femme fatale, embracing grace and subtlety means stepping away from a confrontation, even when you know you are right.

Anger is an unbecoming emotion, one that surfaces during intense exchanges. Sometimes, these debates evolve into personal attacks and harsh words. In such moments, even if your arguments are logical and well-reasoned, it's better to let the dispute fade.

Allowing a loved one to become angry over a heated conversation is beneath the dignity of a femme fatale. By letting go of the need to prove yourself right, you demonstrate poise and maturity, making you more likable in the end.

Tip: When you encounter a fervent disagreement, try to intervene and encourage the parties to find common ground instead of dwelling on their differences. Help them reach a point of understanding so the debate can conclude with elegance and harmony.

Be Grateful

Cultivating a sense of gratitude can be challenging, especially when life presents its cruel, disappointing, and lonely moments. However, as a femme fatale, don't let these difficulties deter you from appreciating what you have and the people who surround you.

Take a moment to acknowledge the blessings in your life, from the small pleasures like a cherished accessory to the more significant ones such as the loyalty and support of your allies.

There is always something to be grateful for and to find joy in. Maintaining this perspective will prevent bitterness from overshadowing your allure and charm.

Tip: Create a list of all the things for which you are grateful, and refer to it whenever life tests your resilience. This practice will keep you grounded and remind you of the power that gratitude holds in shaping your femme fatale persona.

Summary

Embracing humility is essential for unlocking the inner femme fatale, as it allows for growth, learning, and genuine connection. Humility is not about weakness but understanding one's limitations and place in the world.

Key takeaways for practicing humility as a femme fatale include:

1. Allowing others to speak: Give others space to express their thoughts and opinions.
2. Avoiding gossip: Maintain dignity and grace by steering clear of gossip and focusing on meaningful conversations.
3. Overlooking negative actions of others: Cultivate empathy and understanding, and focus on positive qualities rather than faults.
4. Accepting that not everyone will like you: Embrace self-validation instead of seeking approval from others.
5. Backing down from useless fights: Preserve poise and maturity by stepping away from confrontations, even when you're right.
6. Being grateful: Acknowledge and appreciate the blessings in your life to prevent bitterness from overshadowing your allure and charm.

Quality Three

She is Selective

In this section, we'll explore the psychology behind the fear of missing out (FOMO) and how it drives us to want to be involved in social settings. We'll also discuss practical ways to overcome FOMO and become more selective about how we spend our time and with whom we choose to socialize.

As we explore the psychology of FOMO, we'll learn to let go of unhelpful feelings, allowing us to take control of our social life and dating life.

My Story

Once upon a time, not too long ago, I was a very different woman. I was a victim of a sneaky villain called FOMO, or the "fear of missing out." Little did I know that this phantom was the very thing holding me back from my true potential and from unlocking my inner femme fatale.

I was a social butterfly. I had a bustling social calendar filled with events, gatherings, and of course, dates. It seemed like everyone was living a remarkable life, and I wanted a piece of the action. I couldn't bear the thought of missing out on anything that could potentially lead to a fantastic experience or a great connection. The fear of being left behind was so intense that it consumed me.

One Friday evening, I received a last-minute invitation to a party I wasn't particularly excited about. I had been looking forward to a quiet night at home, but the thought of missing out on the potential fun and excitement overpowered my desire for relaxation. Against my better judgment, I put on my party dress, reluctantly applied a fresh coat of lipstick, and headed out the door.

The party was loud and crowded, with people I hardly knew or didn't really care for. As I sipped my cocktail and pretended to be interested in the conversations around me, I couldn't help but feel a nagging sense of emptiness. It was at that moment that I realized I wasn't there because I genuinely wanted to be; I was there because I was afraid of missing out. This fear extended to my dating life as well. I went on countless dates with men I had little interest in simply because I was afraid of missing out on the chance of finding my soulmate. I would say yes to every invitation, even if my gut told me it wasn't right. In my quest to seize every opportunity, I often found myself in uncomfortable situations and unsatisfying relationships. I was needy and desperate for approval, constantly seeking validation from others.

One particularly dismal date stands out in my memory. I had agreed to meet with a man named Jack, who I had met online. Despite our lack of chemistry during our initial conversation, I was determined to give it a chance. As I sat across from Jack at a noisy bar, I realized that I had absolutely no interest in getting to know him. We had nothing in common, and the conversation was painfully dull. But instead of politely ending the date, I continued to feign interest, terrified that I might miss out on a potential love connection.

The turning point came when a dear friend of mine, Maria, confronted me about my FOMO. "Sofia," she said gently, "you're chasing after things that don't truly make you happy. You need to start listening to your heart and figure out what it is that you really want.

Her words resonated with me. I realized that my fear of missing out had been controlling my life and preventing me from discovering my true desires. I needed to take control and make choices based on my own happiness, not on the fear of missing out.

Slowly but surely, I began to change my ways. I turned down invitations to events that didn't genuinely interest me. I declined dates with men I didn't feel a connection with. And most importantly, I started spending more time on my own, learning to embrace solitude and self-reflection. The transformation was remarkable. The more I listened to my inner voice, the stronger and more confident I became. I started attracting like-minded people who shared my passions and interests. I discovered hobbies and pursuits that truly fulfilled me. My newfound confidence and self-assuredness opened doors to a world of experiences that I never knew existed.

I finally understood the true meaning of being a femme fatale. It wasn't about trying to please everyone or being involved in every social event. It was about knowing my worth, embracing my desires, and unapologetically living life on my own terms. By letting go of FOMO, I unlocked the power within me to attract genuine connections and experiences that truly enriched my life.

As I continued on this journey of self-discovery, I noticed a change in my dating life as well. No longer driven by fear, I approached potential partners with a newfound sense of confidence and self-awareness. I knew my worth, and I refused to settle for anything less than what I truly desired. This shift in perspective led me to meet incredible individuals who respected and admired the authentic, fearless woman I had become.

One evening, as I sat at a quaint café sipping my favorite glass of wine, I met Henry. He was charming, intelligent and shared my passion for adventure. Instead of feeling the need to impress him, I allowed myself to be open and genuine. Our connection was undeniable, and it quickly became apparent that we were meant to be in each other's lives.

Now, I stand before you as a woman transformed. I am no longer a slave to FOMO but a true femme fatale who embraces her desires and lives life fearlessly. I've learned the importance of listening to my intuition and making choices that align with my authentic self. And in doing so, I've discovered a world of happiness and fulfillment that I never knew was possible.

The Psychology of FOMO

The modern woman spends an average of 147 minutes per day on social media. As a result, they are more exposed than ever to the curated lifestyles and experiences of others. Every party, romantic getaway, and memorable date is posted for the world to see. For some femme fatales, this constant exposure to the lives of others can lead to the experience of FOMO or fear of missing out.

The phenomenon of FOMO can directly impact mental and emotional well-being in the dating world. Social media is a major catalyst for FOMO, but it is not the only factor. The desire to fit in and belong has been present long before the Internet. This is particularly relevant for femme fatales, who often strive to be part of exclusive circles and maintain a strong social presence. When femme fatales feel as though they are part of an exclusive circle and receive admiration from others, their confidence and self-assurance soar. However, when they don't receive that validation and sense of belonging, their self-esteem may take a hit. It is this hit to their self-esteem that can cause femme fatales to overschedule themselves in pursuit of the perfect dating experiences and social lives.

If you've ever experienced any of the following, you are likely suffering from FOMO:

- **Constantly checking social media:** As a femme fatale, if you find yourself obsessively scrolling through social media to see what others are doing, especially in terms of dating and social events, this may be a sign of FOMO.

- **Overcommitting to social events:** If you notice that you're filling your calendar with events and gatherings you're not genuinely interested in simply because you don't want to miss out, this could be an indication of FOMO.

- **Comparing your dating life to others:** If you're constantly comparing your romantic experiences and relationships to those of others, this may be a sign that you're experiencing FOMO.

- **Fear of making the wrong decision:** If you find yourself hesitant to commit to any plans or relationships due to the fear of missing out on something better, this could be a manifestation of FOMO.

- **Compromising personal values and boundaries:** If you're engaging in activities or relationships that don't align with your core values and principles just to avoid missing out, this is a possible sign of FOMO.

- **Experiencing envy or jealousy:** If you find yourself feeling envious or jealous of the romantic encounters or social lives of others, this could be an indication that you're experiencing FOMO as a femme fatale.

- **Neglecting self-care and personal growth:** If you're prioritizing attending events and pursuing relationships over taking care of your own physical, emotional, and mental well-being, this may be a sign that FOMO is influencing your decisions.

Becoming a Selective Femme Fatale

A sense of belonging and community is essential and beneficial to our mental health. The trick is to balance the pursuit of social engagement with selectivity. If you find yourself experiencing FOMO as a femme fatale try the following:

Remember what you're not seeing on social media: Especially for femme fatales, it's important to remind ourselves that others' dating experiences and social lives aren't as exciting or perfect as they may seem. Keep in mind that people typically don't post the more ordinary aspects of their lives. No one's life is a non-stop thrill ride.

- **Be purposeful with your time:** Focus your energy on relationships and activities that are fulfilling to you as a femme fatale. When you're content with how you're spending your time, you'll be less concerned with how others are spending theirs.
- **Know your triggers:** It can be helpful to identify exactly what is causing you to experience FOMO. Much like any behavioral addiction, understanding and minimizing triggers is important. If your phone is the cause, consider putting it in a different room unless you need to use it. If a specific person regularly triggers FOMO, you may want to limit your time around them.
- **Embrace your inner femme fatale:** Focus on cultivating your unique strengths and qualities as a femme fatale, rather than comparing yourself to others. By building your self-confidence and embracing your individuality, you'll become less susceptible to FOMO.
- **Practice gratitude:** Regularly reflecting on the positive aspects of your life, your relationships, and

your experiences can help combat FOMO. By appreciating what you already have, you'll be less inclined to feel like you're missing out on something better.

- **Set boundaries:** Establish limits on social media use and prioritize self-care, personal growth, and meaningful connections. By setting boundaries, you'll create a healthier balance in your life, reducing the impact of FOMO on your well-being.

Summary

FOMO can negatively impact mental and emotional well-being, causing femme fatales to overschedule themselves in pursuit of the perfect experiences. Key Takeaways include:

1. Signs of FOMO include constantly checking social media, overcommitting to events, comparing your dating life to others, fearing wrong decisions, compromising personal values, experiencing envy, and neglecting self-care.
2. To overcome FOMO, remember what you're not seeing on social media, be purposeful with your time, know your triggers, embrace your inner femme fatale, practice gratitude, and set boundaries in your life. By doing so, you'll create a healthier balance and become a more selective and confident femme fatale.

Quality Four

She Understands the Power of Detachment

In this section, we'll delve into how femme fatales achieve a detached and aloof persona by developing a secure attachment style. A secure attachment style means cultivating emotional intelligence and self-awareness. By understanding our own needs and emotions, we can form connections that are built on trust, intimacy, and mutual respect, without losing our independence and enigmatic charm.

As we explore the journey towards a secure attachment style, we'll learn to balance our individuality with our romantic relationships, allowing us to maintain our captivating allure while fostering deep, meaningful connections with others. This transformation will enable us to fully embrace the magnetic and empowered persona of the femme fatale.

My Story

A few years ago, I found myself besotted by Ben, a charming, kind, and wildly talented musician. Like a moth to a flame, I was drawn to him. The allure of his rock and roll lifestyle and his air of nonchalance captivated me, and I couldn't help but fall head over heels.

Ben wanted to "take it slow" and "keep it casual", but I had other ideas. From the moment we started dating, I had planned our entire life together. During the time we dated, I found myself constantly checking my phone, eagerly awaiting his texts. I obsessively analyzed his social media, looking at photos, who he was tagged with, and working out where he was on the nights he wasn't with me. I'm embarrassed to say this, but I would even cancel plans with friends to make sure I was available whenever Ben had free time, hoping to spend as much time with him as possible. In short, I was needy, clingy, and not at all a femme fatale.

I could feel Ben started to pull away; we saw less and less of one another, and he would take days to text back. One evening I decided to surprise Ben at his apartment. He told me he was feeling unwell and was having a quiet night in. "Perfect," I thought, "this is my chance to show him I care. Show him I'm a real keeper."

I stopped by the supermarket on the way to his apartment, picking up groceries with the intention of cooking him a wholesome meal to make him feel better. But when I arrived at his apartment, I found him having a party with a group of friends. My heart dropped. I felt like an intruder, an outsider in his world. As I stood there, I realized that I had been allowing my insecurities to consume me, turning me into someone I hardly recognized.

Unsurprisingly, Ben and I broke up. I can see now, with full clarity, what went wrong. But at the time, I couldn't understand why.

Sometime after Ben, I met Alex. We met at a coffee shop. Our conversation flowed easily, and before I knew it, I found myself smitten. Our dates quickly escalated from casual coffee meetings to spending almost every waking moment together. I felt like I'd found my other half, and my happiness seemed to depend entirely on Alex.

However, as the honeymoon phase began to wane, I noticed that my insecurities were rearing their ugly heads once more. I found myself constantly seeking reassurance from Alex, asking if he still loved me, if I was enough for him, and if he could ever see himself with someone else. It was exhausting, both for me and for him.

One evening, as I lay in bed questioning my worth once again, I couldn't help but think of my past relationships and how they had all seemed to follow the same pattern. My need for validation, my co-dependency, and my inability to feel complete without a romantic partner. The penny dropped; I was the problem. It wasn't the men in my life; it was me. It was my low self-esteem, my belief that I wasn't good enough. I realized that my fears of abandonment and my need for constant reassurance were holding me back from experiencing the fulfilling, healthy relationships I deserved.

This realization became the catalyst for writing this self-help book, hoping to empower others to uncover their inner femme fatale and break free from the chains of co-dependency and self-doubt.

Attachment Styles

Understanding the power of detachment does not mean being detached. It means knowing when to back off when to let go and being secure enough in yourself to do so. It is about boosting your self-esteem and letting go of your fear of abandonment. Only then can you embrace the femme fatale lifestyle. The way to achieve this "power of detachment" is to look at your "attachment style."

Attachment styles are patterns of behavior that individuals exhibit in relationships, often stemming from early experiences with caregivers. They play a crucial role in how we approach romantic partnerships and can significantly impact our ability to embrace our inner femme fatale. The three primary attachment styles are secure, anxious, and avoidant.

Secure Attachment Style

This is the attachment style that all femme fatales should aim for. Individuals with a secure attachment style are confident in their relationships and feel a strong sense of self-worth. They are comfortable with intimacy, trust their partners, and can navigate both closeness and independence with ease. A femme fatale with a secure attachment style is likely to be self-assured, captivating, and emotionally intelligent. She can maintain a balance between her individuality and her romantic relationships, knowing when to give and receive love while maintaining her independence and allure.

Anxious Attachment Style

An anxious attachment style is characterized by a constant need for validation, reassurance, and closeness in relationships. Individuals with this attachment style may have low self-esteem and fear abandonment, leading to clingy, jealous, and controlling behavior. An individual struggling with an anxious attachment style may find it difficult to maintain her mystique and allure, as her insecurities and need for reassurance can overshadow her natural magnetism. To embrace her inner femme fatale, she will need to address her attachment style and work on building self-confidence and self-worth.

Avoidant Attachment:

Those with an avoidant attachment style tend to distance themselves from emotional intimacy, often fearing vulnerability and closeness. They may appear aloof, independent, and emotionally unavailable in relationships. While a femme fatale may initially appear to possess an avoidant attachment style due to her independence and mysterious aura, a true femme fatale is emotionally intelligent and understands the importance of vulnerability and intimacy in relationships. An individual struggling with an avoidant attachment style will need to work on embracing vulnerability and fostering emotional connections in her relationships while maintaining her independence and enigmatic presence.

Understanding and addressing one's attachment style is essential for anyone seeking to embrace their inner femme fatale. By working on cultivating a secure attachment style, an individual can build the self-confidence, emotional intelligence, and allure necessary to embody the captivating, self-assured, and powerful persona of a true femme fatale.

Becoming a Detached Femme Fatale

Understanding the art of strategic detachment does not mean emotional disconnection. Instead, it entails recognizing when to step back, when to release control, and being confident enough in yourself to do so. Here are some practical approaches to cultivating a secure attachment style for yourself, which in turn creates an enigmatic and captivating aura to others.

Nurture Your Own Talents and Passions

Nurture your talents, passions, and hobbies, immersing yourself in the activities that ignite your inner fire and allow you to live vibrantly. Discovering your passions and the areas where you excel may require patience, but once you find them, you'll effortlessly embody the fearless and captivating essence of a femme fatale. By cultivating your own interests, you'll develop a strong sense of self and independence. This will prevent you from feeling the need to rely on others or tag along in their pursuits. As a result, you'll create a balanced and fulfilling life where you confidently stand on your own two feet, further enhancing your enigmatic and alluring persona.

Embrace Risks

Embrace calculated risks that push you beyond your comfort zone without compromising your safety. Cultivating courage is essential for a femme fatale, and you'll feel empowered as you overcome challenges and realize your untapped strength and resilience. Your newfound empowerment will embolden you to try new things and explore unfamiliar places without relying on others. By confidently venturing into the unknown, you'll continue to grow, learn, and evolve, further solidifying your status as an independent and fearless femme fatale who can navigate any situation with grace and self-assurance.

Work Out and Practice Well-Being

Develop physical strength and well-being, as this not only enhances your allure but also fortifies your mental fortitude. Prioritizing your wellness and self-care fosters emotional stability, allowing you to navigate the complexities of life as a confident and self-assured femme fatale. By building both mental and physical strength, you'll cultivate the inner resilience needed to adapt, the ability to pause when things don't go your way, and be comfortable with giving your partner space when they need it. This balanced approach will enable you to handle life's challenges with grace and composure, further embodying the captivating and self-reliant essence of a true femme fatale.

Practice Self-Kindness

Cultivate self-esteem and self-compassion through introspection and transformation. Pay attention to your inner dialogue, and if you find it critical, consciously replace harsh self-talk with compassion and kindness. Remember, a femme fatale would never treat herself with anything less than the utmost respect, and neither should you. Be mindful that even the most well-versed and cool-minded femme fatale can't have everything go her way. Embrace the fact that life is unpredictable and full of challenges. By being mindful and actively listening to your thoughts, you can gain better control over any clingy or dependent behaviors, allowing you to maintain your captivating and self-reliant persona in the face of adversity.

Summary

In conclusion, embracing a secure attachment style is a vital aspect of embodying the femme fatale persona. By being secure in ourselves, we can be secure in our relationships with others, giving them space when they need it and asking for space when we need it. Key takeaways from the section are:

1. A femme fatale achieves a detached and aloof persona by developing a secure attachment style, which means cultivating emotional intelligence and self-awareness.
2. Attachment styles (secure, anxious, and avoidant) significantly impact one's ability to embrace their inner femme fatale. Cultivating a secure attachment style is key.
3. Embracing detachment involves knowing when to back off and let go, being secure enough in oneself to do so, and balancing individuality with romantic relationships.
4. Practical approaches to cultivating a secure attachment style include nurturing your talents and passions, embracing risks, working out and practicing well-being, and practicing self-kindness.
5. Developing self-esteem, emotional intelligence, and allure are crucial for embodying the captivating, self-assured, and powerful persona of a true femme fatale.

Quality Five

She Sets Boundaries

In this section, we'll explore how femme fatales can effectively set boundaries by refining our communication skills. By confidently expressing our needs, we can establish boundaries that protect our well-being without encroaching upon the rights of others. This enables us to foster and maintain relationships that are not only positive and stress-free but also in alignment with our empowered selves.

As we dive into the art of boundary setting through communication, we'll learn to navigate relationships with grace, confidence, and self-respect, embodying the true essence of the femme fatale.

My Story

This story happened early on in my femme fatale transformation. I had been dressing the part for a while, wearing clothes that flattered my shape, adopting an aesthetic air of glamor and sensuality. Others had noticed the change, and I was starting to attract a lot of attention, but inside I was still the same Sofia; the people pleaser, the pushover, the wallflower. I was someone who would bend over backward just to make others happy. It wasn't enough. Femme fatale is more than skin deep...

It was a sunny summer afternoon, and I had been invited to a friend's birthday party. I had been looking forward to it all week, and I couldn't wait to see my friends and celebrate the special day. I had bought a beautiful dress for the occasion, a bold red number that I thought might help me feel more confident and assertive.

As I walked into the party, I was greeted by an old acquaintance, Jake. He was always the life of the party and had a habit of teasing people, including me. I had never been comfortable around Jake, but I didn't want to make a scene, so I'd always played along with his jokes, even if they made me feel uncomfortable.

He approached me with a grin, saying, "Wow, Sofia, that dress is something else! You're really trying to get some attention tonight, huh?" I felt my cheeks burn, but I laughed it off, trying to hide my embarrassment.

The party continued, and I noticed that Jake kept his attention on me. He made several comments about my dress, my hair, and even my laugh. Each comment felt like a small jab to my self-esteem, but I continued to brush them off, not wanting to upset anyone.

Later in the evening, I went to the kitchen to grab a drink. Jake followed me in and closed the door behind him. He leaned against the counter, blocking my exit. My heart raced as I realized I was trapped in the small space with him.

"Sofia," he said, his tone suddenly serious, "you know, I've always liked you. You're just so... agreeable."

Agreeable?! AGREEABLE?! What kind of a compliment was that? It wasn't a compliment at all, of course. It was a clear indication of how I appeared to others. Agreeable. Placid. Nice. Never stepping on toes and never standing my ground. And now this man thought he could treat me any way he pleased.

I stared at him, unsure of what to say. And even if I had known what to say, would I have said it? I didn't want to lead him on, but I also didn't want to hurt his feelings. I tried to come up with a polite response, but before I could, he leaned in and kissed me.

I froze, my mind racing. I didn't want this, but I didn't know how to say no without causing a scene. He must have sensed my hesitation because he pulled back and looked me in the eye.

"You don't want this, do you?" he asked, his voice almost mocking.

I shook my head, finally finding my voice. "No, I don't."

He laughed, and I could feel my anger boiling inside me. "You never say no, Sofia," he said, stepping aside and opening the door. "I didn't think you'd start now."

I left the kitchen, my eyes burning with tears. As I locked myself in the bathroom, I stared at my reflection, the red dress a stark contrast against my tear-streaked face. I realized then that I had to change. I couldn't let people like Jake control me anymore. I had to stand up for myself, set boundaries, and stop being a people pleaser.

As I looked at myself in the mirror, I realized it wasn't enough to *look* like a femme fatale; I had to *act like one* too. At that moment, I vowed to become a woman who was in control of her life, her emotions, and her relationships.

I had to relearn my behavior patterns, practice assertiveness, and become comfortable with saying "no" when I needed to. I began to realize that my worth didn't depend on pleasing others and that I could stand tall and demand respect.

As I grew into my femme fatale persona, I discovered that not only did I feel more empowered, but I also attracted healthier relationships. People respected my boundaries, and I no longer found myself in situations where I felt uncomfortable or taken advantage of. It wasn't always easy, but with each step forward, I became more confident and self-assured.

Communication Styles

There are three primary communication styles: passive, aggressive, and assertive. Each plays a distinct role in shaping our interactions with others and the way we express ourselves.

Passive Communication

Passive communicators often struggle to express their needs and desires and tend to put the interests of others before their own. As a result, they may experience feelings of resentment and frustration. In the realm of the femme fatale, this style of communication does not align with the empowered, confident persona we strive to embody.

What passive communication sounds like:

- "I'm sorry to bring this up, but..."
- "It's really not important."
- "I don't mind. What do you think?"
- "You probably think this is silly, but..."
- "I'm so bad at this..."
- "Sorry. sorry ..."
- "Am I bothering you? I can come back."
- "Of course I'm not busy; what can I help you with?"
- "I'm probably completely wrong, but ..."

What passive communication looks like:

- Smiles when expressing anger or being criticized
- Fidgets, touches the face, covers mouth with hands
- Raises eyebrows in anticipation
- Speech is hesitant and soft
- Poor eye contact
- Poor posture
- Crosses arms
- Laughs when expressing anger
- Trails off at the end of a sentence

Aggressive Communication

Aggressive communicators forcefully express their opinions and needs, often at the expense of others' feelings and rights. While this style may seem powerful on the surface, it can lead to damaged relationships and a lack of genuine connection. A true femme fatale knows that wielding power does not require steamrolling others.

What aggressive communication sounds like:

- "Don't be stupid."
- "If you don't..."
- "What the hell is wrong with you?"
- "You don't know what you're talking about."
- "You're an idiot / worthless/pathetic."
- "This is clearly too complicated for you, so just do as I say."

What aggressive communication looks like:

- Loud/forceful or sarcastic/condescending tone
- Strong eye contact or staring
- May resort to belittling or even demeaning remarks
- Gestures such as pointing, fist clenching
- Leaning forward or over another person

Assertive Communication

Assertive communication is the golden standard for femme fatales. Assertive communicators express their thoughts, feelings, and needs in a clear and respectful manner, ensuring that their rights are upheld without infringing on the rights of others. This balanced approach leads to healthier, more fulfilling relationships that empower both parties.

As a femme fatale, embracing assertive communication is essential for maintaining control, self-respect, and genuine connections with others.

What assertive communication sounds like:

- "I feel/think / believe..."
- "I would like to ..."

- "What are your thoughts on this?"
- "I don't agree with you on that."
- "How can we handle this problem?"
- "I feel irritated when you interrupt me."

What assertive communication looks like:

- Actively listens
- Speaks clearly and directly
- Good eye contact without staring
- Uses 'I' statements to share thoughts and feelings ('I feel/I think that...')
- Smiles when pleased, frowns when angry
- Offers constructive criticism without blame

Affirmations of an assertive femme fatale:

- "My needs are important, and so are yours."
- "It is my responsibility to get my own needs met. No one owes me anything they haven't agreed to give me."
- "I have the right to express how I feel, and you have the right to disagree."
- "We are equally entitled to express ourselves respectfully to each other."

Becoming a Boundary Setting Femme Fatale

An essential part of becoming assertive and setting boundaries is to recognize what your rights and responsibilities are.

You and others have the right to:

- Say "no"
- Change your mind
- Say, 'I don't know or 'I don't understand.'

- Ask and refuse
- Your own opinion and the right to disagree with others
- Get it wrong, and be responsible for your mistakes
- Offer no reasons, excuses, or justifications for your decisions

For femme fatales, the journey toward assertiveness can vary in difficulty. For some, recognizing our unassertive thoughts and understanding our assertive rights can be enough to replace old beliefs with a more empowered mindset. However, for others, shedding the weight of these ingrained beliefs might prove to be more challenging. For those who need a little extra help, I have provided some assertiveness techniques.

Use "I" statements

"I" statements are a fundamental element of assertive communication for femme fatales. By articulating your emotions, needs, and desires clearly with "I" statements, you assume responsibility and steer clear of placing blame. This approach minimizes defensiveness in others, fostering a more open and receptive atmosphere.

Example:

Aggressive communication sentence: "You never listen to me, and you don't care about my feelings at all!"

Assertive communication sentence using "I" statements: "I feel like my concerns aren't being heard, and it would mean a lot to me if we could work on our communication so that both of our feelings are taken into consideration."

Saying "no" to others

For many individuals, learning to say "no" can be an incredibly challenging feat. However, with practice and refinement, it is a skill that can be mastered. Embracing the power to say "no" without guilt is a valuable habit that femme fatales can develop and incorporate into their assertive communication repertoire.

When femme fatales assertively say "no":

- We take responsibility for ourselves rather than relying on others to do so. This fosters an environment where others feel at ease approaching us with their requests, knowing that we can be trusted to prioritize our own needs and not feel burdened by their requests.
- We demonstrate respect for the other person's ability to handle our refusal, acknowledging their resilience and emotional strength.
- It allows us to enthusiastically say "yes" when we are genuinely able and willing to help, offering our support and time without harboring resentment.
- By setting a precedent for open and honest communication, others will feel more comfortable being truthful with us and declining our requests when necessary. This mutual honesty paves the way for healthier, more transparent interactions.

When saying "no," consider the following:

- Ensure that you have a clear understanding of the specific request being made of you.
- Keep your response concise, unambiguous, and straightforward.
- Refrain from offering lengthy explanations or excessive apologies.

- Embrace your decision without harboring feelings of guilt.

Summary

In conclusion, embracing assertive communication is a vital aspect of embodying the femme fatale persona. By refining our communication skills and setting boundaries, we can foster healthier and more fulfilling relationships. Key takeaways to remember include:

1. Recognize the difference between passive, aggressive, and assertive communication styles, and strive to adopt an assertive approach.
2. Utilize "I" statements to express feelings, needs, and desires without assigning blame or causing defensiveness.
3. Master the art of saying "no" without guilt, taking responsibility for your own needs while respecting the rights of others.
4. Practice assertiveness techniques, such as clarifying requests and providing concise, direct responses.

Quality Six

She is Emotionally Intelligent

In this section, we'll explore how femme fatales can develop emotional intelligence by understanding how thoughts and feelings affect their behavior. By recognizing the link between emotions, thoughts, and actions, the femme fatale can harness their emotional intelligence, captivating and charming those around them.

As we delve into strategies designed to enhance our emotional intelligence, we'll learn the importance of keeping an Emotional Mindfulness Diary (EMD) and how it can help rewire our brain for better emotional awareness and control.

My Story

These days I pride myself on my ability to read people and situations, but looking back, I wasn't always the emotionally intelligent woman you see today. On reflection of my past, I realize that my previously low social intelligence affected many aspects of my life.

One particular incident that still stings is when I made a joke during a group outing with my closest friends. I intended it to be a light-hearted tease, but it ended up driving a wedge between me and my best friend, Lily. We were all out for dinner, laughing and reminiscing about our high school days. Amidst the stories and laughter, I saw an opportunity for a funny comment about Lily's past relationship with a guy we all knew. Unfortunately, my joke came across as insensitive and hurtful, leaving Lily visibly upset. My friends tried to smooth things over, but the damage had been done. I had unwittingly hurt one of the people I cared about most simply because I couldn't gauge the appropriate social boundaries.

As I continued to struggle with my low social intelligence, I found it challenging to maintain strong relationships. I would often forget important dates or overlook the emotions of those around me. One such time, I neglected to remember my dear friend Sarah's birthday.

Sarah and I had been close friends for years, and we shared many happy memories together. However, when her birthday approached, I became preoccupied with my own problems and failed to recognize its significance. I didn't plan anything special or even wish her a happy birthday on the day itself. It wasn't until I saw a photo of her celebrating with other friends on social media that I realized my mistake. My heart sank, knowing that I had let her down. I reached out to apologize, but the damage was done. Sarah felt as though I didn't value our friendship, and our relationship never fully recovered.

My low social intelligence didn't only impact my friendships; it also seeped into my romantic relationships. I remember dating a wonderful man named Alex, who was attentive, caring, and genuinely interested in my well-being. However, I struggled to read his emotions and often misinterpreted his intentions.

One evening, Alex mentioned that he had been spending time with an old female friend from college. Instead of recognizing his honesty as a sign of trust, I became consumed by jealousy. I accused him of being unfaithful and demanded that he stop seeing her. In reality, there was nothing inappropriate about their friendship, but my inability to understand the situation led me to act irrationally.

Our relationship eventually ended, primarily due to my insecurities and emotional outbursts. I couldn't help but wonder how many other relationships I had sabotaged because of my low social intelligence.

Learning to become more emotionally intelligent has transformed my friendships and relationships, allowing me to connect more deeply and authentically with others.

Emotional Intelligence

Emotional intelligence (sometimes called emotional quotient) is the ability to recognize, understand, manage, and use emotions effectively in oneself and others. It involves the following key components:

- **Self-awareness:** Understanding one's own emotions, strengths, weaknesses, values, and motivations. This includes recognizing how emotions can impact thoughts, behaviors, and decision-making.
- **Self-regulation:** The ability to manage and control one's own emotions, particularly in stressful or challenging situations. This includes expressing emotions appropriately, adapting to change, and maintaining a positive outlook.

Emotional intelligence is a crucial skill for embracing one's inner femme fatale, as it empowers individuals to navigate intricate social situations, forge captivating connections, and make astute decisions. Research has demonstrated that femme fatales with high emotional intelligence tend to be more successful in various aspects of life, including romantic relationships, social influence, and personal fulfillment. By mastering their emotions and understanding the feelings of others, they can charm and captivate those around them, becoming the epitome of allure and confidence.

Becoming an Emotionally Intelligent Femme Fatale

It's easy to say, "I need to have self-awareness. I need to regulate my feelings ."But how does one achieve these? It all starts with identifying your feelings, thoughts, and behaviors. By identifying these, you can spot patterns of behavior, change those patterns for the better, and move towards becoming an emotionally intelligent femme fatale.

Feelings

An emotion is a specific feeling that influences how you think and behave. Emotions can usually be described in one word.

Example:

Emma: "I'm dating this guy called Rob, but he hasn't texted me back. It makes me feel _rejected_ and _humiliated_."

Thoughts

Unlike feelings which are just one word, thoughts tend to be longer. Sometimes they are short sentences, and other times they are entire stories we tell ourselves.

We have hundreds of thoughts going through our heads every day; many of them go unnoticed. These thoughts are both a reaction to our emotions and a response to our feelings.

Example:

Emma: "I'm dating this guy called Rob, but he hasn't texted me back. It makes me feel rejected and humiliated. _He's probably getting bored. I'm not good enough. Men only like hot women._"

Behaviors

This is where we start to see how emotions and thoughts affect our behavior, how we feel, and the stories we tell ourselves cause us to act in certain ways. In theory, there is nothing wrong with that; it's just human nature. The issue is if our emotions and stories are out of control, we will act out of control. This results in unwanted behavior that is not emotionally intelligent and not very becoming of a femme fatale.

Example:

Emma: "I'm dating this guy called Rob but he hasn't texted me back. It makes me feel rejected and humiliated. He's probably getting bored. I'm not good enough. Men only like hot women."

In response to feeling rejected and humiliated, and in an effort to make Rob like her again, Emma decides to call Rob on his mobile. Rob doesn't pick up, so she calls him a few more times. He still doesn't pick up, so she texts him. Rob doesn't text back immediately, so Emma makes the decision to visit him after work.

The link between feelings, thoughts, and behaviors is very clear in this example. It's clear how Emma's own low-self esteem has caused her to panic, and as a result, she has told herself a story that may or may not be true. In turn, she has acted in an inappropriate way which will likely scare Rob away. The good news is Emma can rewire her brain and become more emotionally intelligent, and so can you!

Practice Emotional Mindfulness

To help you practice emotional mindfulness and build emotional intelligence, keep an

Emotional Mindfulness Diary (EMD).

I have provided an example of an EMD below to get you started. You can keep your EMD in a physical notebook, on your tablet/laptop, or in a notes app. It just needs to be somewhere you can reach it easily.

I suggest filling out your EMD over six to eight weeks. You should start to see patterns of behavior emerging, which, as embarrassing as it is, will help you in the long run.

Perhaps you will see patterns of neediness when a man doesn't text you back. Perhaps you will see patterns of jealousy when beautiful women talk to your date. Perhaps you will see patterns of gossip when female friends do better than you at something.

It is only when you see these patterns that you can start to change them, and it is only then that you become an emotionally intelligent femme fatale.

TRIGGER	FEELINGS	THOUGHTS	BEHAVIOUR
Everyone thought Catherine was so funny at the party.	Jealous Inferior	I wish I was funny. No one likes me.	I was withdrawn, I didn't talk as much after.
Carlos stopped messaging me on the dating app.	Frustrated Disappointed	What if I said something wrong?	I texted him way too many times when I should have just unmatched and moved on.
Andy took all day to reply.	Anxious Worthless	Did I say something wrong? No one likes me.	I kept checking in on him even though I knew he was probably just at work.
Timothy and I are getting along well and texting a lot after our second date.	Happy Excited Nervous	This is going well. I don't want to mess it up like always.	I've decided I'm going to take it slow and not text constantly. I've noticed texting and not getting replies is a trigger for me, so I should probably work on that.

Summary

This section explored how low emotional intelligence can negatively impact friendships, romantic relationships, and overall well-being. We understand that developing emotional intelligence can help you embrace your inner femme fatale and achieve success in various aspects of life. The key takeaway from this section is:

1. Emotional intelligence consists of self-awareness, self-regulation, and social awareness.
2. Emotions, thoughts, and behaviors are interconnected, and recognizing patterns between them can help you improve your emotional

intelligence.

3. Practice emotional mindfulness by keeping an Emotional Mindfulness Diary (EMD) to identify patterns and work on changing them.

4. Becoming an emotionally intelligent femme fatale requires recognizing and addressing your emotional patterns, ultimately leading to more fulfilling relationships and personal growth.

Quality Seven

She is Unpredictable

In this section, we'll explore how femme fatales can let go of monotony and embrace a spontaneous mindset. By letting go of routine and the tedium that comes along with it, the femme fatale can adopt an aura of unpredictability that is exciting and intoxicating to those around her.

As we delve into strategies designed to embrace our unpredictability and spontaneity, we'll learn the importance of stepping out of our comfort zone and trying new things.

My Story

In the carefree days of my youth, spontaneity was the beating heart of my existence. My friends and I, we were like wildfire, blazing through life with passion and boundless energy. We would dream, dare, and dive into the unknown, with the future nothing more than a distant concern.

I remember one summer evening, as the setting sun painted the sky with hues of gold and crimson, my friends and I decided, on a whim, to embark on an adventure. There were no plans, no blueprints, just the burning desire to embrace life in all its unpredictability. This was not unusual for us; we were in our late teens/early twenties and had little to no responsibilities. This devil-may-care attitude was what we lived by.

We hopped into my old and slightly rusty convertible and set off into the unknown. The wind whipped through our hair, carrying with it the symphony of our laughter and the taste of freedom. We were untamed, wild, and unstoppable.

Our destination was a mystery, even to us. We drove with the moon as our guide, its silver light illuminating the road ahead. Our journey took us through winding roads, dense forests, and sleepy towns until we found ourselves on the edge of the ocean. As the waves lapped against the shore, one of my friends suggested we go skinny dipping. Not caring who saw us, we peeled off our clothes and ran naked into the ocean.

It was a magical time, one where we were ruled by our hearts and not the constraints of society. We were femme fatales without even knowing the phrase yet. We were powerful and enchanting, with the world at our fingertips.

But as the years went by, the spontaneity of my youth began to fade. Life's responsibilities started to weigh me down, and I found myself trapped in the quagmire of routines and schedules. My days became a never-ending loop of tasks, appointments, and obligations. I was a prisoner in my own life.

The spontaneity that had once fueled my existence was now a distant memory, replaced by a numbing monotony that seeped into every aspect of my life. My work, once a source of inspiration and creativity, had become a soul-crushing grind. My social life was reduced to a series of carefully planned outings, devoid of the laughter and excitement that had once been my lifeblood. And my love life? It was a shadow of its former self, just an endless cycle of first-date dinners.

I knew something had to change. I could no longer accept the dullness that had settled over my life like a thick fog. I needed to reclaim the essence of who I was, the femme fatale that had been buried beneath years of responsibility and routine.

Why Unpredictability is Attractive in a Femme Fatale

Unpredictability and spontaneity are considered alluring and exciting for several reasons:

- **Novelty:** Humans are naturally drawn to new experiences, and unpredictable, spontaneous behavior often leads to unique and memorable situations. Novelty stimulates the release of dopamine, a neurotransmitter associated with pleasure and reward, which makes these experiences enjoyable and exciting.
- **Mystery:** Unpredictable and spontaneous people are difficult to predict, creating an air of intrigue and mystery around them. This keeps others guessing, which can be captivating and engaging, as it sparks curiosity and fuels the desire to know more.
- **Break from routine:** Life can become monotonous due to daily routines and responsibilities. Unpredictable and spontaneous experiences provide a refreshing break from the humdrum, allowing individuals to escape the confines of their everyday lives, even if only for a brief moment.
- **Emotional intensity:** Spontaneous experiences often involve risk or adventure, which can heighten emotions and create a sense of exhilaration. This emotional intensity can be intoxicating and create lasting memories.
- **Authenticity:** Unpredictable and spontaneous behavior is often perceived as genuine and unfiltered, as it is less likely to be premeditated or influenced by

societal norms. This authenticity can be appealing, as it conveys a sense of freedom and self-expression.

- **Confidence:** To be unpredictable and spontaneous, a person must have the confidence to take risks and embrace uncertainty. Confidence is an attractive trait, as it demonstrates self-assuredness and a willingness to challenge conventions.

Why Being Unpredictable is Good For You

Embracing spontaneity is good for you, not just the people you're trying to seduce, and here's why: embracing spontaneity has significant positive effects on your emotional health and personal growth.

Psychologists report that unpredictable and spontaneous experiences can enhance a femme fatale's creativity, emotional intelligence, and problem-solving abilities. Furthermore, positive surprises can evoke emotions of trust, love, and joy, releasing "happy hormones" that add to their alluring aura. Experts also emphasize that being open to new experiences enables femme fatales to explore the world and continuously learn, enhancing their mystique.

Breaking free from repetitive cycles and being present in the moment, femme fatales can become more resilient, adaptive, and emotionally strong. By experiencing life without overplanning and allowing themselves to be led by emotions, femme fatales create lasting memories and cultivate a sense of gratitude, making them even more captivating and irresistible to those around them.

Becoming an Unpredictable Femme Fatale

Here are some ways to ease you out of your comfort zone and invite unpredictability and spontaneity into your life.

Look at Missed Opportunities

Recognizing missed opportunities can be an essential step in embracing spontaneity as a femme fatale. Acknowledge those events or experiences you regret not attending to gain insight into your true desires and aspirations.

Take note of the shows, events, or experiences you missed out on in the past. This reflection will help you make values-aligned decisions quickly when spontaneous opportunities arise. As a femme fatale, learning to seize the moment and savor it fully will make you even more captivating and alluring to those around you.

Create an "I Would Love To" List

Dedicate time to making a list of what you truly desire as a femme fatale. Don't take this too seriously; this list serves as tools to help you evaluate your current aspirations and preferences.

Write down every idea that comes to mind without filtering based on cost or time constraints. If something on the list doesn't resonate with you, discard it and start anew. This is not a to-do list but rather an "I would love to" list.

Gaining clarity on your desires allows you to better position yourself to pursue those experiences. Keep this list as your go-to reference when you're in the mood for spontaneity but lack a specific objective in mind.

Schedule Time for Being Unpredictable

It might seem counterintuitive, but even spontaneity requires some planning for those of us with busy lives. Stepping outside your comfort zone and embracing your inner femme fatale demands a different type of energy that must be cultivated—it won't happen overnight.

Allocate a block of time in your schedule, be it an entire day or merely an hour before work, to indulge in whatever you desire. This unstructured time should be flexible and adapt to your unique circumstances. Use this time to explore new experiences, such as reading a recommended blog, visiting a new neighborhood and trying out a local coffee shop, or reconnecting with an old friend.

Incorporating unstructured time into your routine serves as a reminder that playfulness and spontaneity are essential components of the femme fatale persona. It may take some practice to avoid common distractions like email, social media, or your go-to TV show, but be patient with yourself. Nurturing this adventurous and unpredictable energy is crucial for embodying the captivating charm of a femme fatale.

Embrace Imperfection

One of the greatest barriers to embracing your inner femme fatale is fear—the fear of not being perfect, the fear of discomfort, or the fear of others' opinions. This apprehension may prevent you from trying new things and fully immersing yourself in novel experiences.

For instance, you might have turned down a date with a potentially perfect partner because he suggested an activity/place with which you were unfamiliar. Your hesitation to take him up on the offer was the fear of judgment or embarrassment. You see when you're overly focused on perfection, you can miss out on opportunities altogether. It's essential to welcome awkwardness and imperfection as integral parts of the human experience; embracing them can unleash your creative and risk-taking potential.

As a femme fatale, show up and allow yourself to be imperfect in new endeavors. Revel in the process, regardless of the outcome. Over time, you might improve, or you might not. The key lies in enjoying the journey and cultivating the confidence that comes with embracing vulnerability, imperfection, and the allure of the unknown. And if you're too nervous to attend a date/activity in which you fear you might look foolish, revisit your "I Would Love To" list and choose from your pre-selected list of activities.

Summary

In this section, we have explored the allure of unpredictability and spontaneity in the context of femme fatales. Embracing these qualities can lead to personal growth, enhanced creativity, and improved emotional intelligence.

To cultivate this captivating charm, it's essential to break free from routines and allow for unstructured time in your life. This enables you to explore new experiences, face your fears, and embrace imperfections.

As a femme fatale, finding confidence in vulnerability and uncertainty allows you to fully embody this alluring persona and live a more fulfilling, adventurous life.

Quality Eight

She is an Unbothered Queen

In this section, we'll explore how femme fatales can overcome self-doubt and gain control of their thoughts by identifying and addressing unhelpful thinking traps. By recognizing and transforming these limiting thought patterns, we can cultivate an inner confidence that allows us to unlock our Unbothered Queen status.

As we delve into strategies for mastering our minds, we'll learn the importance of self-awareness, positive self-talk, and mental resilience. By adopting these practices, we can embody the true essence of the Unbothered Queen.

My Story

I've started a lot of personal stories so far in this book, but this one might be the most personal of them all. Let me tell you the story of how I became an Unbothered Queen after a trip to Paris with my then-boyfriend, Sam.

Sam and I were in love. We fell for each other hard, and we fell for each other quick. Over the 18 months, we were a couple, we had countless conversations about our dream proposals. One of our favorites was a romantic, moonlit night in a small, quiet café in Paris on a rainy day. We both loved the idea of the rain tapping gently against the windows and the soft glow of candles flickering.

When we finally went to Paris on vacation, my heart was bursting with excitement, and I was sure that Sam was going to propose. We visited all the places we had talked about and did everything we had dreamed of. As fate would have it, on one of those magical Parisian nights, we found ourselves at a quaint café with rain pattering gently against the windows.

I felt the anticipation building inside me, and my heart raced as I thought, "Tonight is the night." But as the night wore on and the rain outside eventually stopped, I realized that the proposal I had been expecting was not coming. My heart ached, and I couldn't help but feel disappointed, angry, and embarrassed.

For weeks after our trip, I spiraled into self-doubt and self-loathing. I thought that I must not be marriage material or even girlfriend material. My inner monologue ruled me, and I was drowning in negative thoughts.

But then, something shifted. I realized that I couldn't continue down this path of self-destruction. It was time for me to rise above my disappointments and take control of my thoughts and emotions. I knew I had to confront my inner critic and learn to live in the present rather than being swept up in fantasies and expectations.

I began to study stoicism and mindfulness, embracing the concepts of living in the moment, accepting the things I couldn't control, and focusing on my personal growth. I read countless books and practiced daily affirmations to help me silence my inner critic.

As I continued on this journey, I slowly transformed into the Unbothered Queen you see today; a woman who lives in the moment and lets go of the thoughts and feelings that do serve me.

Now, I look back on that rainy night in Paris not as a source of heartache but as a turning point in my life. It was the catalyst for my transformation, a necessary step in my journey towards self-love and self-acceptance. I've come to understand that sometimes, we need to face disappointment and heartbreak to find our true strength and resilience.

Focussing on Your Thoughts

It is a sad truth that bad things will happen. Inconvenient things will happen. People will sometimes disappoint us, and life doesn't always go the way we expect. A true femme fatale accepts these things; she feels the emotions, but she rises above them and moves on. This is what I mean when I say an "Unbothered Queen."

So how do we rise above the inconveniences and the disappointments? How do we accept a situation for what it is and not let it rule us? The trick is to change the narrative in our heads. As you read from my story, once I realized Sam wasn't going to propose, I spiraled into self-doubt. Sam was never going to propose, and there's no way to ever change that. What I could change, however, was my response to it.

The way we perceive situations and events greatly influences our emotions and self-image, particularly for those embracing their inner femme fatale. Recognizing and addressing unhelpful thought patterns is the initial step toward adopting a more stoic and balanced way of thinking. Identifying your thoughts may be challenging initially, especially when navigating the complexities of the femme fatale persona. However, with dedication and practice, you will find that mastering your thought patterns becomes an integral part of the Unbothered Queen mystique.

Thinking Traps

"Thinking traps" are patterns in our thinking which lead to negative thoughts. We are more prone to these types of thoughts when we are feeling upset, anxious, or low. Below are some common thinking traps that you may recognize.

Blowing Things Out of Proportion

This thinking trap involves exaggerating the importance of a single incident, causing you to draw sweeping negative conclusions. Be mindful of this tendency and remember that one misstep doesn't define your entire dating experience or your femme fatale persona.

Examples:

- Having a misunderstanding with a date and thinking to yourself, "That's it - they'll never want to see me again."

- Fumbling with your words during a flirtatious conversation and believing that you're terrible at flirting.
- Having a less-than-perfect first date and deciding you're just not cut out for dating or being a femme fatale.

Jumping to Conclusions

This thinking trap is about making negative assumptions based on little or no evidence.

Examples:

- Believing the entire evening is going to be a disaster when your date is five minutes late.
- Going to a party and assuming the man you're talking to thinks you're boring when in fact, he is just shy.

Negative Filter

Seeing only the bad in something or dwelling on negative events instead of positive ones. Explaining away positives for no reason or down to luck.

Examples:

- Having a great day out with your friends, but at lunchtime, your favorite restaurant was fully booked. When you are asked whether you had a good day, you reply, "No. We couldn't get into the restaurant I wanted."
- On being asked out on a date by a good-looking man and thinking, "He probably can't find anyone else to go out with."

Emotional Reasoning

Assuming that because you feel a certain way about something, then it must be true.

Examples:

- Feeling nervous before a date and convincing yourself that you won't make a good impression or that the date will be a disaster.
- Feeling lonely after a quiet weekend and thinking that you're undesirable or not worthy of love and affection.

Labeling

Rating yourself or others with labels based on one situation or incident.

Example:

- Labeling yourself as "undesirable" or "unlovable" after a single unsuccessful date.

Becoming an Unbothered Queen

It can be tricky sometimes to spot your thoughts. You may be in the habit of thinking a certain way, and that makes it hard to step back and review. To help you tackle unhelpful thought patterns, I've provided a useful training exercise I like to call "Catch Your Inner Critic."

Catch Your Inner Critic

The following training exercise is designed to rewire your brain; it will help you identify thinking traps and unhelpful thoughts, retrain your thought pattern, and ultimately help you let go of thoughts that do not serve you.

For a period of six to eight weeks, every time you catch yourself having an unhelping thought, write it down as soon as possible. In addition, think of a more balanced and helpful thought to have in its place. After six to eight weeks, you should start seeing patterns emerging. You will also find that you no longer need to write down the thoughts; you will catch yourself thinking them and start automatically correcting yourself.

UNHELPFUL THOUGHT	BALANCED THOUGHT
Tony hates me.	Tony is acting odd. I don't know why. I should find a way to approach him about it.
I'm fat and ugly.	I am unhappy with how I look right now. What can I do to change that?
Tony said he needs space from our relationship. It's all my fault. I must have done something wrong.	I am upset that Tony wants space, and scared we'll break up. I should use this time to work on myself and decide what I want.
Tony broke up with me. I should give up and die.	It's upsetting, but I deserve someone who wants me as much as I want them.

Summary

The Unbothered Queen is someone who rises above disappointments and takes control of her thoughts and emotions. Key takeaways from this chapter include:

1. Cultivating self-awareness, positive self-talk, and mental resilience helps transform limiting thought patterns and fosters inner confidence.
2. Changing the narrative in your head and your responses to situations are essential for emotional balance.
3. Thinking traps, such as blowing things out of proportion, jumping to conclusions, and negative filters, can lead to negative thoughts and self-doubt.
4. Catching and addressing unhelpful thoughts is vital in rewiring your brain and adopting more balanced and

helpful thought patterns. This can be done through exercises like "Catch Your Inner Critic."

Quality Nine

She Does Not Compete With Other Women

In this section, we'll explore how femme fatales can let go of female rivalry and embrace a mindset of collaboration and support. By acknowledging and addressing our internalized biases, we can work towards fostering a sense of sisterhood that uplifts and empowers all women.

As we delve into strategies for overcoming female rivalry, we'll learn the importance of self-awareness, communication, and mutual empowerment. By adopting these practices, we can embody the true essence of the femme fatale: a confident, self-assured woman who champions the successes of her fellow women.

My Story

Early on in my femme fatale transformation, I found myself at a trendy cocktail party in the heart of the city, dressed to kill in a slinky dress that hugged my curves just right. My confidence was sky-high, and I reveled in the attention I garnered from men and women alike. I couldn't help but feel superior to the other women around me. After all, I was the epitome of a femme fatale, or so I believed.

I distinctly remember the moment I met a woman named Lisa. She was tall, statuesque, and had an air of quiet confidence about her. Instead of celebrating her beauty and grace, I felt a pang of jealousy. I decided that I would be the one to show her who was really on top of the game.

As we chatted, I began to employ my well-practiced tactics of subtle belittlement. I would mention my recent promotion, my exotic travels, and the designer shoes I just purchased. I'd compare her fashion choices to mine, making sure that my tone indicated my superiority. I would laugh at her jokes, but only to follow up with a story that made me seem more interesting and accomplished.

The more I engaged with Lisa, the more I could see her becoming uncomfortable. But instead of feeling victorious, I started to notice how the energy around me had shifted. People were no longer approaching me with admiration but rather with disdain. I realized that my obsession with proving myself superior had not only repelled others but it had also robbed me of the chance to forge a genuine connection with Lisa and the other incredible women around me.

That night, I went home feeling empty and ashamed. I realized that my actions were not those of a true femme fatale. Instead, they were a reflection of my own insecurity and need for validation. I vowed to change, to become a woman who empowers others rather than tearing them down.

A month or so later, on a sunny afternoon, I found myself sitting at an outdoor café with a group of friends. The atmosphere was buzzing with excitement as we were all eager to catch up on each other's lives. It didn't take long, however, for the conversation to take a darker turn.

One of my friends, Marissa, started dishing out the latest gossip about a mutual acquaintance. She gleefully described the woman's failed relationship, her struggle to find a job, and her recent weight gain. The rest of the group leaned in, eager to consume the juicy details. I, too, was initially tempted to join in, but I remembered the bitter lesson I had learned at that cocktail party.

I knew that a true femme fatale doesn't engage in petty gossip or delight in the misfortunes of others. I couldn't let this continue. Instead of indulging in the gossip, I gently steered the conversation toward a more positive topic. I shared stories of inspiring women who had triumphed over adversity, and the group slowly began to follow suit.

As the conversation shifted, I noticed the energy at our table change. The air of negativity dissipated, and we were all suddenly more focused on lifting each other up and celebrating our successes. We left the café that day feeling empowered, our bond as friends stronger than ever.

Looking back on these two anecdotes, I realize that a femme fatale is not just a woman who knows how to seduce. She understands the power of celebrating other women and rising above the need to impress.

Female Rivalry in Society

As a femme fatale, you need to understand that true power doesn't come from competing with other women or keeping them down. In fact, femme fatales thrive by lifting one another up and celebrating the strength and confidence of all women. Unfortunately, not all women understand this. Let me share some personal experiences from other women in my life who have experienced women not supporting other women:

"In my professional life, I once had a female manager who tried to silence me by instructing me not to voice my opinions or ask questions during meetings."

"I faced a situation where a female colleague plagiarized my work and took credit for my contributions in a report."

"On one occasion, I confided in a female peer about a challenging client I was dealing with. Instead of offering support, she went to

my boss and twisted my words, saying I was having trouble building relationships."

In yet another tale, I encountered a vibrant young woman at my dance studio who shared her experience of applying for a transfer at her workplace only to be passed over. She discovered that the department in question already had one woman on the team and "didn't want another." Frustrated by this exclusionary attitude, she took matters into her own hands and sought out a more inclusive company. While not everyone has the privilege to make such a move, her decision to stand up for herself by "voting with her feet" not only enhanced her self-assurance but also led her to a better professional environment.

It's evident that the mindset of women undermining other women is distasteful, but we must recognize that the women involved are not the sole culprits. Studies have demonstrated that women often internalize the patriarchal narratives that they are less capable, competent, and strong than their male counterparts. This phenomenon is known as internalized sexism.

Subconsciously absorbing these societal messages about their designated roles, women may end up projecting these beliefs onto one another. This can manifest in the mistreatment, underestimation, and alienation of other women as they strive to elevate their status and gain recognition among men.

Furthermore, traditional notions of successful leadership have largely been shaped by male standards. With limited female role models to look up to, professional women have often found themselves emulating men in order to gain acceptance and advance in their careers and social lives.

To determine whether you might be unintentionally competing with other women, take a moment to reflect on the following questions:

- Do you find yourself judging other women for decisions that don't align with your own choices?
- Are you more inclined to criticize women for minor missteps while overlooking significant faults in men?
- Do you tend to dismiss men's behavior by attributing it to "just the way it is"?
- In your interactions with female colleagues, do you notice a stronger inclination to compete rather than collaborate?

By honestly examining your thoughts and actions, you can identify any areas where you may need to shift your mindset and embrace a more supportive approach toward other women.

Becoming a Supportive Femme Fatale

Here is a list of practical ways you can embrace the femme fatale attitude of building up other women:

- Instead of judging a struggling woman, lend a helping hand and share your own experiences.
- Amplify other women's voices in social settings by reinforcing their ideas and suggestions. If a woman is interrupted, encourage her to finish her thought without directly calling anyone out.
- Recognize and publicly praise women's contributions, ideas, and achievements.
- Refrain from gossiping or speaking ill of other women. Offer constructive feedback directly and respectfully.

- Challenge sexist remarks or jokes, even if they aren't directed at you. A simple statement like "I didn't find that funny" can help disrupt inappropriate behavior.
- Abandon double standards when judging female friends and acquaintances, including yourself. Assume good intentions and seek understanding when confronted with puzzling behavior.
- If you've achieved success as a femme fatale, support and uplift other women without subjecting them to the same obstacles you faced. Extend a helping hand.

Summary

Embracing a femme fatale mentality encourages women to rise above competition and focus on empowering and supporting one another. This mindset involves lifting other women up, celebrating their strengths, and fostering collaboration rather than rivalry. Femme fatales prioritize amplifying women's voices, offering mentorship, building relationships, and challenging societal norms that perpetuate sexism. By adopting this mentality, women can break the cycle of female rivalry and contribute to a more inclusive and supportive environment for all.

In addition, by adopting this approach, you will appear more confident, self-assured, and influential while simultaneously inspiring other women to embrace their own power and potential.

Chapter 6

The Secrets of Dark Feminine Seduction

Secret One

Choosing Your Target

The art of seduction starts with identifying the type of person you want to attract and the relationship you desire. Just as a painter selects the right canvas and colors for their masterpiece, so too must you carefully choose your target. In this first secret of feminine seduction, we'll explore how to determine what you're looking for, what you value in a potential partner, and where to meet them.

First, ask yourself what kind of relationship you're interested in. Are you looking for a casual one-night stand, a more relaxed friends-with-benefits arrangement, a committed partner, or a lifelong husband? Knowing the answer to this question will not only help you clarify your intentions but also guide you in selecting the right person to fulfill those desires.

Next, take the time to reflect on what you value in a partner. Remember, a femme fatale is a woman who is confident in her desires and knows what she wants. Consider traits such as physical appearance, intelligence, sense of humor, and other personal qualities that you find attractive. Don't shy away from being specific; the more detailed your vision, the easier it will be to recognize the right person when they cross your path.

Once you have a clear idea of what you're looking for and what you value, it's time to identify where you might meet this person. Different environments will cater to different types of relationships and potential partners. For instance, if you're looking for a casual encounter, you might find success in bars or clubs where people are open to meeting new people and having a good time. However, if you're looking for a long-term partner, going to a club where a group of men are at a stag party might see you with a broken heart.

If you're searching for a more serious relationship or even a future husband, consider places where people share your interests and values. This could be anything from joining a local sports league to attending art classes or participating in a book club. By surrounding yourself with like-minded individuals, you increase your chances of finding someone who is compatible with you.

Of course, don't overlook the power of online dating and social media platforms. These modern tools provide an endless sea of potential matches and can be especially useful for busy femme fatales who may not have the time to socialize as much as they'd like. Just remember to be authentic and honest in your online interactions, and don't be afraid to let your inner seductress shine through.

The first secret of feminine seduction is all about choosing your target. By knowing what you want, identifying what you value in a potential partner, and selecting the right environment to meet them, you set the stage for a successful and empowering seduction. As you continue to unlock your inner femme fatale, remember that confidence, clarity, and intention are your greatest allies on this journey.

Secret Two

Give Him the "Je Ne Sais Quoi" Syndrome

"Je ne sais quoi" is a French phrase that translates to "I don't know what" in English. It is often used to describe an indefinable, mysterious quality that makes something or someone captivating and irresistible. In the context of feminine seduction, cultivating your own "je ne sais quoi" means using everything you have learned so far.

A femme fatale knows her strengths and doesn't shy away from showcasing them. Whether it's your wit, intelligence, or talent, let these attributes shine through in your interactions with others. This will not only make you more attractive but also demonstrate that you are comfortable in your own skin.

Next, practice the art of subtlety. Sometimes, less is more. A coy smile, a gentle touch, or a lingering gaze can speak volumes and create an air of mystery around you. By revealing just enough to pique your target's interest without giving everything away, you can keep them guessing and longing to know more about you.

Focus on building a strong sense of self. A woman with a "je ne sais quoi" knows who she is and isn't easily swayed by the opinions of others. She has her own unique style, preferences, and beliefs, which make her all the more intriguing. By cultivating your individuality, you can ensure that you stand out from the crowd and leave a lasting impression on those around you.

Finally, remember that an air of mystery isn't just about what you say or do—it's also about what you don't say or do. Mastering the art of silence and leaving room for interpretation can be a powerful tool in creating a "je ne sais quoi" aura. Be careful not to overshare or reveal too much about yourself too soon. Instead, allow your target to gradually discover different aspects of your personality, maintaining an enigmatic appeal that keeps them coming back for more.

A little method I have cultivated over the years is; when I meet a man, and I can tell he's interested, it doesn't matter how much I like him, when he asks me for my number... I say no. I give him my Instagram instead. Why? Firstly, because I can do a little stalking, check if he's the right man for me, and get an idea of his interests. Second, it also gives me space from him; I choose when I give him my number, and I control how and when (and if) we move forward. The trick, of course, is saying it in such a way that doesn't cause him offense or cause him to think you're not interested. So imagine this; he says, "Can I get your number?". I raise an eyebrow, give a coy smile, look him up and down, bite my lip, and in a soft tone, I reply, "You can have my Instagram ."If he gets defensive or questions me too hard, then I tell him to take it or leave it. I have expressed my boundary, and if he actually likes me, he'll have picked up on the hints that I like him too.

Secret Three

Unveiling the Art of Keeping Him Addicted

In the world of dating and seduction, it's not uncommon for a man to pull back from time to time, whether due to external circumstances or a need for personal space. As a femme fatale, it's essential to understand how to handle these situations and stay in your feminine energy, ensuring you maintain your allure and keep him addicted.

It's essential to examine your feelings and reactions when a man pulls back, especially in situations involving casual relationships such as friends with benefits. If your friend with benefits is seeing other women and you find yourself experiencing jealousy, you can't blame him for needing space. You expect him to give you the grace of seeing other men, so why are you not affording him the same situation?

Being a femme fatale means knowing what you want, and if you're experiencing jealousy in this situation, it may be time to reevaluate what you truly want from the relationship. Are you truly comfortable with a casual, non-exclusive arrangement, or do you desire something more serious and committed? Be honest with yourself about your feelings and needs. If you realize that you're seeking a deeper connection or exclusivity, you have two choices; talk to him about it, or continue being miserable. If your man is only interested in a friends-with-benefits situation, you need to accept that and walk away with elegance.

However, if it's a long-term partner who is pulling away, the approach is different. In this instance, it's crucial to consider your boundaries, self-respect, and personal values. A strong and self-assured woman knows her worth and will not tolerate being treated poorly or disrespectfully.

If your partner's withdrawal is causing you emotional distress or violating your boundaries, it may be time to reevaluate the relationship. Be gracious and poised, and if necessary, make the decision to end the relationship yourself. By taking control of your own happiness and well-being, you demonstrate your self-respect and self-worth.

Once you've made a decision to leave, focus on moving forward with your life without resentment or bitterness. Avoid airing your dirty laundry or engaging in negative gossip about your former partner. Instead, invest your energy in nurturing your passions, interests, and friendships. This not only helps you heal but also showcases your strength, resilience, and unwavering grace in the face of adversity.

In many cases, when a femme fatale ascertains and maintains her boundaries, it causes the man to return, realizing the value of the connection he had with her. However, during the time apart, you may have grown emotionally and discovered that you no longer desire him in the same way. This newfound clarity and confidence will empower you to make the best decision for yourself, whether that involves rekindling the relationship or moving on to new opportunities.

The important thing to remember is that, regardless of the outcome, you now have the ball in your court. By knowing when to back off and when to allow space, you have demonstrated your strength, self-respect, and understanding of healthy relationship dynamics. As a result, you are better equipped to navigate future relationships with grace and poise, maintaining your alluring and irresistible feminine energy.

Secret Four

How to Rise Above the Manipulation Game

It's crucial to understand that true femme fatales are not toxic or manipulative. They embody confidence, self-assurance, and allure without resorting to harmful or deceitful tactics. Unfortunately, some people may confuse the concept of a femme fatale with manipulative behavior, leading them to adopt unhealthy and damaging strategies in their pursuit of seduction and attraction. In this section, we'll discuss how to rise above the manipulation game and embrace the authentic power of a femme fatale.

Recognizing these behaviors will empower you to respond effectively and maintain your independence. Some common manipulative behaviors to watch out for include:

- **Guilt-tripping:** Manipulators may use guilt to make you feel obligated to comply with their demands or wishes. They may try to convince you that you're responsible for their emotions or problems, making it difficult for you to assert your own needs or desires.
- **Gaslighting:** Gaslighting is a form of psychological manipulation in which the manipulator causes you to question your own perception of reality. They may deny the truth, twist facts, or outright lie to make you doubt your own memories, experiences, or judgments.
- **Playing the victim:** Manipulators often play the victim to elicit sympathy and gain control over others. They may exaggerate their problems, blame others for their misfortunes, or refuse to take responsibility for their actions in order to manipulate your emotions and make you more susceptible to their influence.
- **Using flattery or charm:** Manipulators may use flattery, compliments, or charm to disarm you and make you more susceptible to their influence. While there's nothing wrong with receiving or giving compliments, be wary of those who use them excessively or insincerely to gain your trust or favor.
- **Emotional blackmail:** Emotional blackmail involves using threats, intimidation, or negative consequences to force someone to comply with their demands. This

could include threatening to end a relationship, withholding affection, or even using physical violence.

- **Diverting attention or blame**: Manipulators may try to divert attention away from their own actions or behaviors by shifting the focus to someone or something else. They may use this tactic to avoid taking responsibility for their mistakes or to shift the blame onto others.

By recognizing these manipulative behaviors, you can avoid falling into their traps and maintain your independence. As a femme fatale, it's essential to protect yourself from toxic influences and stay true to your values and beliefs. With a keen awareness of manipulation tactics, you can confidently navigate the complexities of relationships and maintain your self-respect and alluring charm.

Secret Five

Be Authentic

A true femme fatale embraces her authenticity and remains true to herself rather than trying to be someone she's not or pretending to have it all together. She does not follow trends or compare herself to others, understanding that her unique qualities are what make her captivating and irresistible. This secret is all about cultivating a strong sense of self and embracing your individuality.

Embrace your uniqueness! Recognize and celebrate the qualities that set you apart from others. Whether it's your sense of humor, creativity, or intelligence, embrace these attributes and let them shine through in your interactions with others. By doing so, you'll create an alluring aura that draws people in and leaves a lasting impression.

To be truly authentic, it's essential to know yourself well. Spend time reflecting on your thoughts, emotions, and values to gain a deeper understanding of who you are and what you stand for. This self-awareness will guide you in making decisions and navigating relationships that align with your true self.

Remember to stay true to your values and beliefs. A femme fatale knows what she believes in and remains true to her values, even in the face of opposition or societal pressures. By standing firm in your convictions, you demonstrate integrity and strength, which are both attractive and empowering qualities.

It's ok to be vulnerable and open. Authenticity involves being open and vulnerable, allowing others to see the real you. This doesn't mean oversharing or revealing your entire life story but rather being genuine and honest in your interactions. By doing so, you'll build trust and form deeper, more meaningful connections with others.

Most importantly, don't compare yourself to others. Remember that other women are not more attractive than you; they just *think* they are and *act* like they are. Comparisons only serve to undermine your self-confidence and distract you from embracing your unique allure. Focus on developing your own self-worth and cultivating your individual strengths, and you'll naturally exude an irresistible charm that sets you apart.

Conclusion

In this book, we've explored the essence of the femme fatale, teaching you to embrace your full feminine energy to transform your dating, love life, and relationships. By understanding the history, mythology, and evolution of the femme fatale, you've learned to balance your dark and light feminine energies to unlock your full potential.

Using evidence-based psychology from cognitive behavior therapy, attachment theory, and self-improvement therapies, we've guided you in fostering true and lasting change from within. We've emphasized that genuine transformation goes beyond mere aesthetics or mimicry of behaviors, focusing on tapping into your authentic self.

I will take this time to remind you of the importance of embracing both dark and light feminine energies. Both are necessary and in your pursuit of power, do not forego your softer side. By embracing both light and dark sides of yourself, you are making changes to the stuffy societal expectations and redefining what it means to be a woman.

As you reclaim your rightful place as a powerful, magnetic, and seductive being, I encourage you to go into the world as a bold, daring, sensual femme fatale.

A Message To The Reader

As an author, there's nothing more fulfilling than knowing that my book has touched someone's life in some way. Your support and encouragement mean everything to me, and I'm deeply grateful for each and every one of you who have taken the time to read my book.

I would like to kindly ask those of you who have read my book to consider leaving a review on the platform where you purchased it. Your honest feedback helps other readers decide whether or not to give my book a chance, and it also helps me to grow and improve as a writer.

About the Author

Sofia De Paulo is a talented author and passionate advocate for women's empowerment. Born to a Spanish mother and an American father, she spent her formative years in both Spain and the United States. She now resides in Los Angeles, where she is working on her latest book.

De Paulo is an avid gardener, wine taster, and Bachata dancer, but her true passion lies in helping women embrace their feminine energy. Sofia's previous experience owning a dance studio has given her a unique perspective on the challenges that many women face in today's world, and through her studio, she has helped hundreds of women connect with their bodies and feminine energy with grace and fluidity.

De Paulo's body of work provides a comprehensive view of feminine energy, both light and dark. She believes that both sides are essential to achieving balance in life, and her writing reflects this belief. Her approach is compassionate and encouraging, and her books provide practical and inspiring advice for women who are looking to connect with their feminine energy.

Her books are not just a guide for women; they are also a reflection of De Paulo's own journey. She knows firsthand what it feels like to be trapped in a masculine world, and she has used the techniques outlined in her books to help herself and other women find balance in their lives. She believes that every woman has the potential to step into her feminine power and live a life that is fulfilling and joyful.

Sofia De Paulo is a gifted author and advocate for women's empowerment. Her body of work explores the power of feminine energy, both light and dark, and provides practical tools and techniques for women to connect with this energy. Her compassionate and encouraging approach has won her many fans, and her work continues to inspire women around the world to embrace their feminine power.

Printed in Great Britain
by Amazon

34607220R00078